DIGITAL REVOLUTIONS
Activism in the Internet Age

About the author

Symon Hill has been an activist since his teens. He has campaigned for causes including religious liberty, disability rights, equal marriage, economic justice and alternatives to militarism. He has trained hundreds of people in media activism. He is an associate of the Ekklesia thinktank and an associate tutor at the Woodbrooke Quaker Study Centre. He co-founded Christianity Uncut, a network of Christians campaigning against the UK government's cuts agenda.

Symon formerly oversaw media relations for the Campaign Against Arms Trade (CAAT) and was involved in taking the UK government to court over arms sales to Saudi Arabia. As a result, he was nominated as a Hero of 2007 by the activist comedian Mark Thomas in the *Independent on Sunday*. In 2012, he was dragged by police from the steps of St Paul's Cathedral during the eviction of Occupy London Stock Exchange. His first book, *The No-Nonsense Guide to Religion*, explored religion in its social and political context. He lives in London.

Acknowledgements

I am conscious that this book covers a vast range of campaigns and issues. I could not possibly have personal experience of all of them. Naturally, I have greater knowledge about the campaigns that I have personally been involved in, the country I live in and the people with whom I am in contact. Having sought out activists in other movements and from elsewhere in the world, I hope I have represented them fairly and done justice to their experience. I owe many thanks to everyone who agreed to be interviewed and who discussed the issues with me, as well as to the writers, campaigners, bloggers and academics on whose thoughts I have drawn.

Particular thanks go to my editor, Chris Brazier, and his colleagues at New Internationalist. I owe many thanks to Hannah Brock, who gave immensely helpful feedback and support throughout the process. Thanks also to Adam Kirk Smith, Deborah Grayson, Nicola Sleap and Chris Wood, whose comments on individual chapters helped to improve them. The mistakes are all mine.

I owe just as many thanks to my friends and family who were so patient and supportive as I worked on the book and who helped me to keep calm and focused. I could not have written this book without them. Thanks to the staff of cafés in southeast London and beyond, who tolerated my buying very little while I worked for hours on my laptop.

Most importantly, I am grateful to the people who first encouraged me to become an activist and to all those who have supported me and campaigned alongside me since then. I would not be an activist, let alone a writer, without you.

Symon Hill

DIGITAL REVOLUTIONS
Activism in the Internet Age

Digital Revolutions: Activism in the Internet Age
First published in 2013 by
New Internationalist Publications Ltd
55 Rectory Road
Oxford OX4 1BW, UK
newint.org

Design: Ian Nixon
Imprint editor: Chris Brazier

Printed by T J International Limited, Cornwall, UK who hold environmental accreditation ISO 14001.

MIX
Paper from
responsible sources
FSC
www.fsc.org   FSC® C013056

British Library Cataloguing-in-Publication Data
A catalogue record for this book is available from the British Library.

Library of Congress Cataloging-in-Publication Data
A catalog record for this book is available
from the Library of Congress.

ISBN: 978-1-78026-076-1

Contents

For additional material (full transcripts of interviews, articles, blogs and updates) visit the Digital Revolutions page at **www.newint.org/books**

Foreword

by **Peter Tatchell**

Digital revolutions do not make social revolutions in and of themselves. It is not the technology itself that brings down repressive regimes, exposes unjust laws, frees political prisoners or secures human rights. Social change comes from the people – the people on the ground who are using digital technology, as well as more traditional methods, to help organize and expand their demand for change.

We witnessed the digital revolution as an aid to social revolution during the Arab Spring and the protests against the rigged presidential elections in Iran and Russia. It has also been adapted to great effect by the anti-austerity and Occupy movements in Europe and America.

But, as Symon Hill writes, technology can be both an instrument of reform and a means of resisting reform: 'The internet has been a tool, not a cause, of social change. It has profoundly affected the way people communicate. It has made it easier for people to see the truth that the powerful would rather hide, to learn from activists on the other side of the world, to co-ordinate campaigns without hierarchy and to expose governments and corporations to public ridicule. It has also helped those same governments and corporations to spy on activists, to disrupt campaigns, to spread their own messages through well-funded advertising and to create an illusion of popular support.'

One of the most telling passages in this book is the section about 17th-century republican agitators taking advantage of the latest printing technology to spread the anti-royalist message via pamphlets. As Symon Hill reveals, people who want to change the world for the better have always made use of the latest technology, from the printing press to the tweet.

My own campaigning, which is now into its fifth decade, has evolved to reflect this. I began in my hometown of Melbourne, Australia, in the late 1960s – campaigning for Aboriginal rights and against the death penalty and the Vietnam war. It was an era before computers, photocopiers, home printers, mobile phones, video cameras, the internet and social media. Using a manual typewriter, I used to type the text of leaflets and news releases on to waxed paper, wrap it around an inked drum and then hand crank a slow, laborious, messy duplicating machine to print them out.

News releases to the media had to be posted or delivered by hand – often in the middle of the night to make sure they were on the news desk first thing the next morning. Protest photos needed to be sent away for developing and printing, which took at least three days.

Having begun with these primitive, archaic methods, I've since embraced with enthusiasm successive waves of new technology, from my first computer to photocopiers, fax machines, mobile phones, email, digital photography, websites, Facebook, Twitter and so on. These technological innovations have extended the reach and effectiveness of my activism.

Nowadays, like other campaigners, I email my news releases and photos instantly to subscribers, journalists and other human rights organizations – reaching 15,000 people at the click of a mouse.

Within hours of my attempted citizen's arrests of President Robert Mugabe in 1999 and 2001 I was able to email a news release and photo links worldwide; helping to ensure global media coverage of Mugabe's human rights abuses and my bid to bring him to justice.

I have two websites: my personal one (PeterTatchell.net), which, as well as human rights, also includes political, green and animal rights issues; and the strictly human rights website, PeterTatchellFoundation.org Via these two cyber platforms, people worldwide – from New York to Beijing, Santiago and Harare – can learn about my campaigns.

Individuals anywhere can – and do – access the advice section on the Foundation website. It offers practical, hands-on information to victims of asylum refusal, harassment, discrimination, hate crimes and police malpractice – wherever they live.

By reading my Facebook posts, 9,000+ people – scattered over many different countries – can see immediately the wide range of humanitarian causes I am working on and get involved if they wish. This has been really useful in mobilizing people to sign petitions and email government leaders in protest against the anti-gay repression in Iraq, Nigeria, Belarus and Cameroon.

Via Twitter, the 30,000+ people who follow me receive regular 140-character comments, information and links to news, campaigns and photos. It has proven invaluable as a way to alert people instantly to the latest massacres in conflict zones such as Balochistan, Somalia and West Papua.

All in all, my email and social-media outpourings reach nearly 50,000 people. I don't have to rely solely on the mainstream media any more. I am a publisher and news outlet in my own right.

From my experience, it is clear that any campaigner who wants to have an impact and make a difference needs to engage with the world using the latest technological platforms. Social media make it so much easier to spread the word about human rights abuses and to inform the media, organize protests and lobby governments. When two young men were thrown out of the John Snow pub in London in 2011 for kissing, a protest campaign was very quickly mobilized on Facebook and Twitter. It led to hundreds of people joining a kiss-in outside the pub and to masses of media coverage about the discrimination this same-sex couple had experienced.

The same goes with the campaigns to free arrested democracy, trade union, student and ethnic-minority activists in Iran, Russia, Pakistan and Zimbabwe. Within hours, news of their arrest can be spread worldwide and e-petitions can gather hundreds of thousands – sometimes millions – of signatures from the global online community.

The downside is that this clicktivism is seen by some people as a quick-fix substitute for the longer, harder slog that is often required to secure social change. It's great to sign a petition against Uganda's Anti-Homosexuality Bill. This adds to the pressure on the government in Kampala. It is also very important that people email their MPs or members of Congress. But winning the battle for equality in Uganda – and everywhere else – involves much more. This includes research to document injustices, the drafting of alternative policies, briefing journalists and politicians, delegations to meet government ministers, picketing the perpetrators of injustice and so on.

My own campaigning has often involved direct action, which has many times got me arrested and beaten up, as happened at the attempted Moscow Gay Pride in 2007. Cyberactivism is not enough. Sometimes, it is necessary to put your own body on the line.

As this book points out, the opponents of democracy and equality are just as capable of using social media as we are. This is what happened with the campaigns against same-sex marriage in the UK and the US. Homophobic religious leaders mobilized their supporters to swamp legislators with petitions and letters in opposition to marriage equality.

Symon Hill devotes a whole chapter to explaining some of the sophisticated, manipulative digital techniques corporations and governments have used to further their own agendas – and to undermine critics and protests. In many countries, there have been organized internet campaigns by the far right to disparage and subvert efforts to secure racial, gender and sexual orientation equality. Indeed, I have been on the receiving end of lots of online hate campaigns, and even death threats, organized by supporters of rightwing extremist organizations like the British National Party and the English Defence League, as well as by Islamists and apologists for the Mugabe and Putin regimes. Rightwingers are getting social media savvy, as well as leftwingers.

Although Facebook, Twitter and other new internet technologies have their limitations, overall they are positive developments, traversing national boundaries, circumventing state censorship and creating global communities online.

Symon Hill's engaging book – clearly written and accessible – talks good sense: the internet offers tools for resistance and change that all activists need to deploy to secure success in the modern online age. But these cyber tools are a means to an end, not an end in themselves. They alone can never bring social and political change. People are the key force for changing society – here and worldwide. Technology can help us achieve this change but ultimately it is we, the people, who make history.

Peter Tatchell
Australian-born British campaigner for human rights
PeterTatchell.net

Introduction

In 2008, an economic crash exposed the truth of a system in which the wealthy benefit and the rest of us pay for it. But the rest of us have fought back. Since 2008, and especially since 2010, the world has been rocked by the power of the have-nots acting together. Dictators, corporations and elected governments were taken by surprise in the face of the power from below. From Mexico City to Madrid, from Hong Kong to Cape Town, protest camps sprang up in public squares. The '99%' demanded that the '1%' give up control. Three dictators fell in north Africa. Activists put corporate tax dodging on the mainstream political agenda. A global movement challenged attitudes to sexual violence. Israel and Quebec saw the biggest protests in their history. Greece came closer to electing a radical leftwing government than any country in the European Union since it was formed. In the face of popular protests, the Chinese government reversed a policy on energy and Saudi Arabia gave the vote to women.

This is not to say it has been easy. Regimes such as Bahrain and Syria have unleashed unimaginable levels of terror on their own people. European and North American governments have responded to the economic crisis by demanding that the poorest should pay for it. Relatively democratic countries have seen an increase in police violence and harsh sentences for protesters. Corporations have continued to wield unaccountable power. And of course, for all the global movements and successes we hear about, there are many more campaigns that fail to make much impact.

The years following 2010 have been compared to the uprisings in central and eastern Europe in 1989, to the global wave of protests in 1968, to the 'great unrest' of 1910-14 and to the revolutions of 1848. Historians will be writing about these movements for centuries. They will debate many of the questions that are now being asked, along with others that we cannot imagine.

Few questions about this global outbreak of activism raise as much controversy as the role of the internet. There are cyber-utopians who attribute the Arab Spring, Occupy Wall Street, anti-austerity campaigns and other global movements entirely to technology. Some eagerly speak of a 'Facebook revolution' or 'social media revolt' with little if any reference to the economic factors and human complexities that have triggered unrest, protest and change. It seems bizarre to see technological change as a bigger cause of the recent outbreak of activism than the global economic crash that it immediately followed. This is not to say that the crash was the only factor. The social movements of recent years have been varied. They have been influenced by complex historical and cultural factors. However, the economic situation has been the trigger for many of them and we won't get very far by talking about cyberactivism without taking into account the role of economics.

As James L Gelvin puts it in his book on the Arab revolts, 'Attributing the uprisings to social media transforms the protagonists into patsies who act not because they choose to but because they are are somehow technologically compelled to'.[1] It also implies that the real credit for social change should go to the heads of transnational corporations such as Facebook and Twitter, rather than to the millions of people who have bravely stood up to oppression.

At the other extreme of the debate are those who think that the internet has made no difference at all. The writer Evgeny Morozov, who has made a career out of denying that the net is a tool of liberation, dismissed the importance of social media in the Tunisian revolution even as Tunisians were saying how vital it had been.[2] Some even argue that the internet is undermining activism. Jonathan Heawood, director of the Sigrid Rausing Trust for promoting human rights, says that 'Twitter and other social networks have given people the impression that fighting for human rights is easy: all you have to do is hit "retweet" and the world will be a better place.'[3] This argument implies that there are large numbers of people sitting at their computers who would be out on the streets protesting were it not for the invention of Twitter. To say the least, this seems unlikely. Recent years have shown that many people are sufficiently angry, realistic and courageous to realize that protesting online is not enough on its own. The thousands who braved the cold to camp in public squares, the many more imprisoned and tortured from Beijing to Riyadh and the nonviolent protesters who gave their lives in Bahrain and Egypt are hardly examples of lazy activists.

Heawood is right to recognize that there are millions of people who sign online petitions but take no further action. But it is doubtful that they believe that this alone is changing the world. It is likely that many of them would take no political action at all were it not for the internet. Rather than deterring people from activism, the internet has drawn people to it.

Take British student Adam Whybray, who signed up to give a monthly donation to Amnesty International and to receive emails about their campaigns. He told me that an email about Troy Davis, a US man about to be executed after what Amnesty regarded as an unfair process, 'really struck a nerve with me'.

He explains: 'After signing a petition and encouraging friends on Facebook to do so and informing my family, I was inspired to attend the campus Amnesty meeting about the case.' He decided to become involved in activism 'in the real world', joined protests over tuition fees and 'really grasped that the personal is the political'.[4]

The internet has been a tool, not a cause, of social change. It has profoundly affected the way people communicate. It has made it easier for people to see the truth that the powerful would rather hide, to learn from activists on the other side of the world, to co-ordinate campaigns without hierarchy and to expose governments and corporations to public ridicule. It has also helped those same governments and corporations to spy on activists, to disrupt campaigns, to spread their own messages through well-funded advertising and to create an illusion of popular support.

There are a number of academic books that explore in intricate detail the role that technology plays in life and politics today. This is not one of them. It is a book about grassroots activism. In particular, it is about the activism that has swept the world since the crash of 2008. While describing the movements involved, I have tried to give space to the voices of those who took part in them, so that their experiences and views take priority over analysis by me or by others. Inevitably, I have faced difficult choices about which movements and campaigns to include and have left out more than I would like. At various points, the book pauses to ask, what was the role of the internet? What would have been different without it? Has it been a tool of power or counterpower, of liberation or control? The book is a snapshot of activism and the internet in a short but significant space of time.

The first chapter looks at the development of cyberactivism by the time of the economic crisis and the ways in which governments and citizens responded to that crisis. Chapter 2 considers how the internet and mobile phones have threatened the powerful by the release of information, particularly through filming disputed incidents. Chapters 3, 4 and 5 look at recent global movements – the Uncut protests, the Slutwalks, the uprisings in north Africa and the Middle East, the Indignados and the Occupy camps. Chapter 6 asks how the internet helps to make small-scale campaigns more effective and how it can both empower and disempower marginalized groups. Chapter 7 explores the ways in which corporations use the net to resist protest and how activists are fighting back. Chapter 8 offers some thoughts on the future of grassroots activism in the age of the internet.

I have sought to illustrate my conclusions with examples. When writing the book, I occasionally became bogged down in theory and had to remind myself that activism is as diverse as the people who take part in it. The book does not focus on technological campaigns led by presidential candidates or the revelations of organizations such as Wikileaks, important though they are. It concentrates on the mostly unknown people who choose to stand up and unite in the face of injustice. The core principle with which I have approached the book is not a belief about the internet but a conviction about power: liberation comes from below and never from above.

The aspects of freedom and justice that we enjoy today are due to the commitment of millions of people down the centuries whose names we will never know. More freedom and greater justice will come about because of millions more people in the present and the future who choose to challenge unjust and oppressive systems. *Digital Revolutions* is dedicated, with thanks, to them all.

1 James L Gelvin, *The Arab Uprisings*, Oxford University Press, 2012. **2** Evgeny Morozov, 'First thoughts on Tunisia and the role of the internet', ForeignPolicy.com 14 Jan 2011. For further discussion on this point, please see Chapter 4. **3** Jonathan Heawood, 'There's more to protesting than "retweet"', *The Independent*, 20 Aug 2012. **4** Adam Whybray, interviewed 18 Feb 2012.

The 'menace' of cyberspace

Social media and other communication technologies have been a feature of recent protest movements. The mainstream media moved from ignoring them altogether to presenting them as revolutionary. But just how central has the internet been to recent resistance?

'Iran's Twitter revolution' announced the headline of a *Washington Post* editorial as thousands of Iranians marched against their government in 2009'.[1] 'The revolution will be twittered,' echoed Andrew Sullivan of *The Atlantic*.[2] British Prime Minister Gordon Brown declared: 'This week's events in Iran are a reminder of the way that people are using new technology to come together in new ways to make their views known.' He insisted that, because of the internet, 'foreign policy can never be the same again'.[3] The media was full of talk of how the internet could bring about political change.

Fast forward 18 months and things looked rather different. Protests broke out across Tunisia, with those involved sharing information and encouragement on Facebook. The US and British media initially paid little attention. The BBC did not cover the Tunisian uprising on its website until more than a week after it began.[4] Nir Rosen of New York University tweeted about his frustration with 'shitty Western media ignoring uprising in Tunisia and regime's brutal crackdown'. Pointing out that Tunisia's government was friendly to the US, he wrote that the public would hear a lot more 'if it was in Iran'.

As the Tunisian police opened fire on demonstrators and millions poured onto the streets, even the BBC and CNN could no longer ignore the situation. When Tunisian dictator Ben Ali fell from power, there was excited talk about a revolution brought about by the internet. Some found it a convenient explanation – much easier than analyzing economic causes or addressing the complicity of Western governments in oppressive regimes. For others, it provided genuine and passionate hope for the defeat of oppressive forces worldwide. Wael Ghonim, one of the most prominent activists in the Egyptian revolution that followed the uprising in Tunisia, insisted that 'this is the internet revolution'.[5] In contrast, another prominent Egyptian activist, Gigi Ibrahim said: 'When they call ours a Facebook or an internet revolution – that's just bogus.'[6] Who's right?

Utopia and dystopia

When communication changes, other changes become more likely. The invention of the printing press around 1440 gave vastly increased numbers of people access to books. It took a while for printing technology to become widely available, but as it spread across Europe, the Bible and other influential writings were translated from Latin and Greek into common languages. The Church's monopoly on the scriptures was broken as more people began to read and interpret them for themselves. It would be simplistic to suggest that the invention of the printing press directly caused the Reformation that began about 80 years later. But it is reasonable to think that the Reformation would not have taken place without it, or at least not in the form in which it did.

By the mid-17th century, the cost of printing was coming down. In England, the price plummeted in the early 1640s as social unrest and then civil war broke out. The English revolution led to the execution of King Charles I in 1649 and the creation of a short-lived republic. By this time, varied radical groups were promoting their causes through mass-produced pamphlets. In turn, their opponents printed pamphlets attacking them.[7] After the monarchy was restored in 1660, one of the first acts of the new government was tightly to restrict the production of printed newspapers. Critics of the regime managed to circumvent the printing law by copying out large numbers of news-sheets by hand, employing speed-copyists to get them into coffee houses as quickly as possible. Then as now, activists would use whatever means of communication were available. Novelty and surprise have been tools of resistance for a long time.

As technology developed in the 19th and 20th centuries, new forms of communication provoked heated debate about their merits. Jenny Pickerill of the University of Leicester says that 'Many technologies have, with time, been treated similarly, from the telegraph to the television. First there is utopian excitement tinged with dystopian gloom, and then criticism and complexity.'[8] Radio, television and computer games were all attacked by people who said that children would spend too much time with them and not enough time with their family or engaged in healthy exercise. Radio and television allowed journalists to put politicians on the spot with difficult questions that helped the public to form their own opinions. Of course, they also helped governments to convey their own messages and private companies to pay for advertisements that promoted not only their products but the values that encouraged people to buy them.

In 1969, two US universities managed to link up computer networks through a system that came to be called the arpanet. More universities were gradually added in the following years and similar systems developed in Europe. The term 'internet' dates back at least as far as 1974. In 1990, the world wide web was launched, allowing internet users to access websites posted anywhere in the world. Now the terms 'internet' and 'world wide web' are often used interchangeably, but are not in fact the same: technically, the internet hosts the web. The last restrictions on the internet to carry public traffic were removed in 1995.

It was around this time that the internet began to impact on public consciousness, at least in relatively rich countries. Some 21 per cent of the US population had access to the web in late 1997, although access levels elsewhere were generally much lower.[9] The same year, US President Bill Clinton mentioned the internet six times in his State of the Union speech. This should not be taken as a sign that politicians were familiar with technology. It was later claimed that Clinton had never used a computer in his life, while French President Jacques Chirac was overheard asking what a computer mouse was called.[9]

At that time, the web was often treated as something mysterious and exotic. Indeed, the mainstream media remained suspicious of it for some years. Some saw a threat to their own monopoly on reporting news, while others felt genuine concern about the spread of inaccurate information and unverified claims. Others resorted to mockery and disdain.

British journalist Emily Bell describes a popular attitude towards the internet in the late 1990s:

'The "real world" of mainstream media began to gravitate around the most logical and probably the least defensible position it could: that the internet was a conduit for the perverted, the distorted and the untrustworthy. This network of limitless connectivity which might, with the most limited imagining, be the single most empowering publishing technology since Gutenberg invented the printing press, was instead vilified as a home of the con artist and the paedophile… At the heart of this collective suspicion seemed to be a belief that anyone who used the internet for almost any purpose at all was almost certainly up to no good.'[10]

Such perceptions were fueled by pseudo-scientific claims. In 1995, *Time* magazine ran a story about the dangers of 'cyberporn'. It cited a study from Carnegie-Mellon University that claimed that the majority of images accessible on the internet were pornographic. The report, which turned out to be based on the work of an undergraduate called Marty Rimm, was immediately discredited by a range of scholars. Donna Hoffman and Thomas Novak from Vanderbilt University insisted that pornography accounted for less than half of one per cent of images posted online. Rimm's methodology was found to be woefully inadequate. In the end, even Carnegie-Mellon University backed down and apologized, but that did not stop the claims sticking in the public mind.[9]

Some criticized the internet as the preserve of an élite, while others passionately tried to make it more widely available. The US writer Howard Rheingold expressed his anger with the prejudices that associated the internet with pornography, pointing out that marginalized groups may be among the greatest beneficiaries:

'Here are a few people to talk to about the menace of cyberspace: The Alzheimer's caregiver afraid to leave the house who dials in nightly to a support group; the bright student in a one-room Saskatchewan schoolhouse researching a paper four hours from the nearest library; the suicidally depressed gay teenager; AIDS patients sharing the latest treatment information; political activists using the net to report, persuade, inform; and the disabled, ill and elderly, whose minds are alive but who can't leave their beds. For them and for potentially millions of others like them, cyberspace is not just a lifeline, it can be better than the offline world.'[11]

New departure

The internet was already being used for political activism in the early 1990s, when the Zapatista movement in Mexico published their aims online and peace activists in the Balkans used the net to communicate across enemy lines.[12] Indeed, several scholars have argued that the Zapatistas were responsible for beginning a change in global politics by demonstrating the potential of the internet.[13]

Some campaigners were quicker to get on board than others. In 1997, Friends of the Earth encouraged supporters with email access to send emails to world leaders attending the United Nations Climate Change summit in Kyoto.[8] It was one of the first incidences of what has become a very common practice. It was not until 1999 that much of the mainstream media began to notice cyberactivism. 'Internet message sets off a rampage' declared a headline in the UK after a minority of protesters at an anti-capitalist protest damaged property.[8] The authorities were thrown by the use of the web to organize resistance. 'Virtual chaos baffles police,' declared *The Observer*.[14] In scaremongering tones, the rightwing *Daily Express* said that web-based organizing was 'a new departure for protest' – and they didn't mean it in a positive way.[15] Here was a fearsome new movement whose leaders could not even be identified. As similar protests continued in Britain, the Conservative opposition called for anti-capitalist demonstrations to be banned.[16]

Across the Atlantic, tens of thousands of activists gathered outside a meeting of the World Trade Organization in Seattle – and closed it down. The 'Battle for Seattle' drew global attention as police clashed with protesters. The campaigners had their own media teams, who posted information online as well as liaising with mainstream media. This was the beginning of Indymedia, an international network of citizen journalists reporting about social and political issues online. Leah A Lievrouw of the University of California describes Seattle as a 'watershed moment' for cyberactivism.[12] The watershed may have at least as much to do with mainstream media becoming aware of cyberactivism as with changes amongst activists themselves.

The Battle for Seattle was certainly a key moment for what was inaccurately labeled the 'anti-globalization movement'. Those who belonged to it tended to prefer the term 'global justice movement'. They were protesting against the globalization of corporate power. It was becoming increasingly clear that campaigns could not be confined within nation-states. By 1999, the majority of the world's 100 biggest economies were corporations rather than countries.[17]

In 2001, US President George W. Bush launched the so-called 'war on terror'. The focus for many activists was diverted to peace campaigns. Peace and environmental campaigns often tended to operate separately, with many of the latter using the internet in organizing the global Climate Camp movement, which involved protest camps at governmental meetings and power stations. In 2003, when Jenny Pickerill conducted one of the first major academic studies of cyberactivism in Britain, she found that attitudes to internet campaigning still tended to be either 'utopian or dystopian'.[8]

Slowly, an appreciation of complexity began to appear. By the middle of the decade, mainstream media were starting to take the web more seriously, partly due to the presence of younger journalists who had been communicating online for longer than they had worked in the media. It was also becoming obvious that the web could be a good source for news, not least in countries that journalists found difficult to access. After the US invasion of Iraq in 2003, a number of Western journalists turned to websites from within Iraq to help them gain a clearer idea of realities on the ground. The word 'blog' – short for 'weblog', an online diary – became well-known as journalists increasingly used the more popular blogs as a source of information, or at least to find out about a diversity of opinion. By 2006, there were estimated to be 27 million blogs worldwide.[10]

The middle of the decade saw 'color revolutions' in southwest Asia and eastern Europe. They were so called because the resistance movements identified themselves by wearing particular colors, as with the 'orange revolution' in Ukraine and the 'rose revolution' in Georgia. There was much talk of the role of the web in allowing activists to organize their resistance. While the role of the web in the color revolutions was almost certainly exaggerated, it pushed web-based activism further up the media agenda.

Subsequent years saw an explosion of 'social networking sites' – websites that aimed to help people communicate and share information and photos with friends and colleagues. The most famous, Facebook, was originally designed for students. This did not stop it being used for politics. For example, when British university lecturers took industrial action in 2006, students at University College London joined rival Facebook groups of supporters and opponents of the action. Later that year, the site was made available to the general public. The same year saw the launch of Twitter as a 'microblogging' site, allowing users to send messages of up to 140 characters to those who chose to 'follow' them. The first billion tweets had been sent by 2008.

A key moment for cyberactivism, as well as for internet history generally, was the introduction of the video-sharing site YouTube in 2005. As mobile phones became cheaper and more common in much of the world, many included cameras. With more computers able to play sound, phones able to record brief films and a site available on which people could easily watch them, the stage was set to send images around the world that would once have remained hidden.

According to the International Telecommunications Union, the number of internet users increased from 2 per cent of the world's population in 1997 to 35 per cent in 2012. The figures for 2012 varied considerably from country to country – from less than one per cent of the population in Burma, Sierra Leone and North Korea to over 95 per cent in Iceland.

Unsurprisingly, richer countries tend to have the highest rates of access while poorer countries have the lowest. The highest rates are found mostly in northwest Europe, North America and parts of southeast Asia. Some of the lowest are in central and southern Africa – and other parts of southeast Asia. The middle range includes most countries in Latin America, which has access rates of around 40 to 50 per cent, comparable to parts of eastern and southern Europe.

All these figures should be treated with caution. While telecommunications companies can estimate levels of internet access, it is very hard to produce precise figures for numbers of users. This is particularly so in areas where much of the use takes place in internet cafés and on shared computers, as in many of the countries involved in the Arab Spring.

Money and power

No amount of technical knowledge or internet history can explain the global outbreak of activism that followed 2008, and intensified from 2010. The economic crash of 2008 is a far more important explanation than any technological development.

It is accepted wisdom that nobody saw the crash coming and nobody expected the Arab Spring or other cases of global activism. This is not true, however. Few people within political and media establishments may have predicted them, but they were not listening to the warnings outside. In Britain, for example, The Corner House, a social-justice research group, had been warning of economic meltdown for some years. The Oxford Research Group, which explores alternative approaches to conflict and security, had predicted a 'revolt from the margins'.

In 2008, it became clear to the public that something was very wrong. Bankers had gambled with money that they did not own. Politicians had let them get away with it. Newspapers had failed to question them. It did not take a degree in economics to realize that the system was rotten. It was time for society to take stock and think about how to create a better system.

That, of course, is exactly what didn't happen. A number of governments bailed out banks without making them publicly accountable. They introduced austerity measures to pay off debt, effectively demanding that the poorest people and those in the middle should pay for a crisis that the rich had done most to cause. The very wealthy were largely unaffected. In 2008, the year of the crash, boardroom pay in the UK increased by 55 per cent.[18] In 2009, the three richest individuals in the world owned $112 billion between them.[19] The European Union demanded cuts to public services and the welfare state in return for bailouts to Greece, Ireland and Spain.

Canadian writer and activist Naomi Klein was among those who accused the very rich and the political right of using the crisis for their own benefit. She said: 'When people are panicked and desperate and no-one seems to know what to do, that is the ideal time to push through their wish list of pro-corporate policies: privatizing education and social security, slashing public services, getting rid of the last constraints on corporate power.' She added that this was happening 'the world over'.[20]

Austerity – and therefore protests – took longer to reach some countries than others. As early as 2008, campaigners in Italy marched with the slogan 'We won't pay for your crisis'. The same chant was later heard in Greece and gradually across Europe. The first European country to experience mass protests was Iceland, whose people were hit hard because of the particular position of Icelandic banks. The Icelandic police used pepper spray against demonstrators for the first time in 60 years. In January 2009, protesters banged pots and pans to drown out a speech by the Prime Minister. The country's media immediately dubbed it a 'kitchenware revolution'. Later in the year, Icelandic voters elected one of the most leftwing governments in Europe, many of whose members had backed the protests (three years later, Iceland's economy was more stable and equitable than most of Europe).[21]

Meanwhile, the US launched a policy of 'quantitative easing', effectively a euphemism for creating money. The result was massive inflation overseas, particularly in the Global South. By the time crowds of protesters gathered in Egypt in 2011, food prices in the country had rocketed by 19 per cent in a year. Youth unemployment stood at 30 per cent in Tunisia, 46 per cent in Spain and 50 per cent in Yemen.[22]

In February 2011, with protesters marching in Athens, shops occupied in London and the Egyptian people on the verge of defeating a dictatorship, the BBC's Paul Mason wrote a now famous blog entry called 'Twenty reasons why it's kicking off everywhere'.[23] It provoked heated debate and triggered a book of responses.[24] A few months later, Mason developed his arguments in a book, *Why It's Kicking Off Everywhere*.[22] He points to a change in 'the demographics of revolt', as younger populations in several countries (particularly in north Africa) coincide with economic decline and unemployment, producing 'graduates with no future'. Because of the internet, he argues that 'for the first time in decades, people are using methods of protest that do not seem archaic'. He talks of the breakdown of hierarchies, enabled by the spread of the internet and mobile phones, and the rise of the 'networked individual'. A part of his argument that is sometimes overlooked is about changing relationships between classes, as a number of factors lead 'the radicalized middle class, the poor and the organized workforce' to build alliances.

All these points are relevant and behind them all is the reality of the economic crisis. I know several people who responded to Mason's title by saying 'I know why it's kicking off everywhere!' before going on to express their anger about food prices, bank bail-outs and austerity. To be fair to Mason, he is not denying this. Rather, he is going into more detail. Nonetheless, economics are overlooked surprisingly often when discussions start about the internet's role in activism. However much we discuss technology, let's not do so in a way that leads us to forget the slums in Egypt, the soup kitchens in Greece or the newly present food banks in Britain.

Power from below

The cause of the recent global activism has been economic, not technological, but this does not mean the internet has been irrelevant. The Iranian sociologist Farhad Khosrokhavar rightly says that 'there is no causal link between social protest and communication technologies'. But he is equally right to add that 'technologies change dramatically the way people interact and build up groups and alliances... bringing in new dynamics that would have been absent without them'.[25]

The activist writer Tim Gee points out that the powerful generally exercise their power in three ways.[17] First, there is idea power. The dominant way of looking at the world is reflected in films, books, newspapers, advertising and political debate. Then there is economic power. The very rich are usually the ones with the most power. They have the upper hand in determining wages and prices and tend to have more influence over government when it comes to policies on business and tax. Finally, there is physical power. Governments, armed forces and sometimes corporations can, if they choose, impose their will through force and even violence.

Of course, power is a complex thing. Gee's analysis is a rough model, but nonetheless helpful for that. Against these forms of power is the power from below – counterpower. Idea counterpower can be used by those who reject dominant values and spread different ideas through word of mouth, the media – or the internet. Physical counterpower is seen when people literally get in the way of the powerful. Examples include blocking access to a military base or power station, conscientious objectors who refuse to kill and acts of mass non co-operation. Strikes, boycotts and divestment affect the pockets and bank balances of the powerful and are forms of economic counterpower.

Gee argues that 'Many of the most successful movements for transformational change have used all three kinds of counterpower, while many of those that have fallen by the wayside have used only one or two.'

The internet is relevant to all three types. It can be used to organize economic and physical resistance as well as to spread alternative ideas. Its interactive nature gives it advantages over other forms of communication, but it has its weaknesses too. Critics of cyberactivism often say that the majority of the web still promotes dominant values. This is a good argument against seeing the internet as entirely different from other media. It is not a good argument against using the net as a tool of counterpower.

The majority of books, films and magazines also uphold dominant values, but almost no-one argues that books, films and magazines cannot also be used to resist them. It would be naïve to regard the internet as wholly liberating when the leading websites are owned by huge corporations and the most popular news sites are those linked to existing media outlets and broadcast networks.[26] But it would be irresponsible for activists to neglect something that is proving so useful at mobilizing counterpower. The internet does not create resistance, but it can both encourage it and affect the form that it takes.

When resistance happens in new ways, élites can be taken by surprise. When communication takes new forms, control over communication can be weakened or broken. Institutions reliant on traditional forms of communication are slow to realize the potential of new ones. The next chapter takes two examples from shortly after the economic crash, when events revealed that very different governments had underestimated the power of citizens to use new technology against them.

1 'Iran's Twitter revolution', *Washington Times*, 16 Jun 2009. **2** Andrew Sullivan, 'The revolution will be twittered', *The Atlantic*, 13 Jun 2009. **3** Gordon Brown, interviewed in *The Guardian*, 20 Jun 2009. **4** 'Tunisia security forces shoot dead protester', BBC online news, 25 Dec 2010. **5** Wael Ghonim, 7 Feb, quoted by Lin Nouiehed and Alex Warren, *The Battle for the Arab Spring*, Yale University Press 2012. **6** Phil England, 'Fear no more: Power of the People' (interview with Gigi Ibrahim), *New Internationalist*, May 2011. **7** See Christopher Hill, *The World Turned Upside Down* (Penguin, 1991) and Andrew Bradstock, *Radical Religion in Cromwell's England* (IB Tauris, 2010). **8** Jenny Pickerill, *Cyberprotest: Environmental activism online*, Manchester University Press, 2003. **9** John Naughton, *A Brief History of the Future: The origins of the internet*, Phoenix, 2000. **10** Emily Bell, 'Fact-mongering online' in *Where the Truth Lies*, edited by Julia Hobsbawm, Atlantic Books, 2006. **11** Howard Rheingold, quoted by Naughton, *op cit.* **12** Leah A Lievrouw, *Alternative and Activist New Media*, Polity Press, 2011. Thanks to Nick Wilson Young for the information about the Balkans. **13** Andrew Chadwick, *Internet Politics*, OUP 2006. **14** 'Virtual chaos baffles police', *The Observer*, 20 Jun 1999. **15** *Daily Express*, 19 Jun 1999. **16** Carolyne Culver, 'Crackdown on the cards after May Day violence', *Tribune*, 5 May 2000. **17** Tim Gee, *Counterpower*, New Internationalist 2011. **18** Owen Jones, *Chavs*, Verso, 2011. **19** Derek Wall, *The Rise of the Green Left*, Pluto Press, 2010. **20** Naomi Klein, 'The most important thing in the world', 6 Nov 2011, reproduced in *Dreaming in Public: Building the Occupy movement*, edited by Amy Schrager Lang and Daniel Lang/Levitsky, New Internationalist, 2012. **21** Bernadette Meaden, 'The Icelandic alternative', *Ekklesia*, 20 Sep 2012. **22** Paul Mason, *Why It's Kicking Off Everywhere*, Verso, 2012. **23** Paul Mason, 'Twenty reasons why it's kicking off everywhere', BBC blog, 5 Feb 2011. **24** Alessio Lunghi and Seth Wheeler (eds), *Occupy Everywhere*, Autonomedia, 2012. **25** Farhad Khosrokhavar, *The New Arab Revolutions that Shook the World*, Paradigm, 2012. **26** James Curran, Natalie Fenton & Des Freedman, *Misunderstanding the Internet*, Routledge, 2012.

2

Breaking the monopoly

2009: in Iran and Britain two individual deaths are transformed by social media into events of massive political significance. And both governments and media barons realize the game has changed.

Women scream. Police attack peaceful protesters with batons. People run away. The police come from different directions at once. There is a confused image of feet as protesters run into each other. There are more screams and the sound of weapons on skin. In a split-second glimpse of humanity, a policeman hesitates to bring down his baton a second time. There is more shouting, more confusion, more beating. The film of the incident, recorded by a protester on a phone, is less than a minute long.

Filmed at Vanak Square in Tehran, it was one of many images to appear on YouTube during the Iranian protests of 2009.[1] As Paul Mason put it, 'If it had been taken by a TV cameraman, that 58-second single shot would have won awards. It captures reality in a way you rarely see on TV news.'[2]

The internet beamed the reality of the Iranian protests into homes and workplaces around the world. Iran was not the only country in which cameraphones and YouTube were challenging government repression and police violence. With phones becoming cheaper, more computers now able to play sound and the existence of websites on which to watch them, the stage was set for the worldwide sharing of images that powerful people would rather were not seen.

The effect was gradual. In Burma in 2007, nonviolent resistance by Buddhist monks was readily viewable around the world, despite the regime's tight control on communication. Examples from two countries in 2009 – Iran and Britain – show how much their governments had failed to learn from these cases. Political and media élites in both countries were confronted with a painful truth in 2009: their monopoly on communication had been broken.

Technological fools

On 1 April 2009, national leaders from 20 countries assembled in Britain for the latest meeting of the G20. Thousands of activists gathered outside the Bank of England in central London. It was only months since banks had been bailed out. Feelings about the financial system were running high. With the presence of so many national leaders in the British capital, the police were nervous. The date of the meeting was a gift for protesters. Trade unionists, climate campaigners and anarchist groups all drew on the imagery of April Fools' Day to present the world's leaders as 'financial fools' or 'climate fools'.

I can vividly remember the relaxed atmosphere outside the Bank. The sun was shining, banners were waved and people sang. Then the police over-reacted. They decided that the protesters should not be allowed to leave. They were 'kettled' in a small area near the Bank – surrounded by riot police who gave them little room to move. There were no toilets, or anywhere to buy food or drink. Several protesters combined practical need with symbolic action by relieving themselves against the wall of the Bank of England.

The word 'kettled' is appropriate. The atmosphere declined rapidly, as tempers rose and boiled over. In a key tactical error, the police decided that not even journalists should be allowed out of the kettle. The next day's papers contained reports by people who could see why the mood had changed. When people tried to leave, the police pushed them back. Later in the day, a passer-by called Ian Tomlinson collapsed and died after being knocked to the ground by a police officer. At a demonstration the next day, protester Nicola Fisher was viciously beaten across the leg by a police sergeant.

While the UK technically has a free press, the media is dominated by the power of a few 'media barons' who own the majority of newspapers. Most push a rightwing agenda. In the past, they rushed to defend any police officer accused of brutality. The protesters in question would be smeared, with suggestions that it was they who had been violent.

This time, the reaction was different. Mobile phone cameras and the internet made the usual approach almost impossible. The attacks on Tomlinson and Fisher were filmed and posted on YouTube. It was obvious that neither of them had been violent. To measure the impact of new technology, we only have to compare these attacks with previous allegations of police assault. The new situation reached its most bizarre moment when Nicola Fisher sold her story to the rightwing *Daily Express* – although the paper was keen to blame a 'rogue' police officer and to defend the police as a whole. [3]

The most widely witnessed death in history

Two months later, on 13 June 2009, Iranian President Mahmoud Ahmadinejad was declared re-elected. The authorities said that he had received 62 per cent of the vote.

Within hours, protesters were on the streets. Widespread reports of ballot-rigging were fueled by apparent turnouts of more than 100 per cent in two districts. The leading opposition candidate Mir-Hussein Mousavi refused to accept the result. His supporters marched down Tehran's Valiasr Street chanting 'Mousavi, take back my vote!'.

And they filmed it. Before long, videos shot on mobile phones were appearing on the internet. Opposition supporters used

Twitter to publicize protests. Western journalists who were barred from Iran relied heavily on social media to find out what was going on.

It was not only violence that was filmed. An anonymous protester with the YouTube name of 'Oldouz84' broadcast poems from rooftops. Rooftop protests had quickly taken off, with campaigners calling out 'Allah-hu-Akbar', a phrase much used by Muslims, which roughly translates as 'God is great'. In one video, Oldouz84 insisted that 'Allah-hu-Akbar' was 'no longer about being a Muslim' but had become a call to resistance from people of all faiths. 'It's a call to unity, whether Muslim, Jew, Zoroastrian, faithless or faithful,' she insisted. 'Too many children will not hold their parents tonight. It could have been you or me.'[4]

On 20 June, a week after the disputed election result, an unarmed 26-year-old Iranian protester called Nedā Āghā-Soltān was shot dead by a pro-government militia member. Three separate videos of the incident appeared almost immediately on YouTube. They show the shooting, Āghā-Soltān's last words as she lay dying and – only moments later – her death itself. *Time* magazine suggested it was 'probably the most widely witnessed death in human history'.[5]

The context of the Iranian protests was very different from the anti-G20 demonstrations in London two months earlier. What was similar was the way in which public footage affected the establishment response. To begin with, the Iranian government attempted to prevent the death being discussed. It was alleged that they had tried to stop public mourning for Āghā-Soltān and prevent mosques from holding collective prayers in her memory.[6] Several attempted memorial gatherings were organized by anti-government protesters and reportedly dispersed by the authorities.

Before long, the government response changed. The presence of three eyewitness videos, seen by millions around the world, meant the Ahmadinejad regime could not simply wait for the incident to be forgotten. Just as the rightwing media in Britain had been unable to deny that Nicola Fisher and Ian Tomlinson were peaceful, the YouTube footage prevented the Iranian authorities from portraying Nedā Āghā-Soltān as a violent protester. She had done little more than step out of her car at the time she was shot.

Instead, the regime and its supporters resorted to conspiracy theories, most of which contradicted each other. The Iranian ambassador to Mexico, Mohammad Hassan Ghadiri, was one of the first to take this route. Less than a week after the shooting, he suggested that the CIA could have killed Āghā-Soltān in order to whip up hostility to the Iranian government.[7] He argued that 'the bullet that was found in her head was not a bullet that you could find in Iran'. In fact, Āghā-Soltān was shot in the chest, not the head, as the videos make clear and the doctor at the time testified.

Ghadiri said he was suspicious of the videos, questioning how they could have been shot so clearly and effectively. The next week, Ezzatollah Zarghami, the head of Iran Broadcasting, insisted that the videos were made by the BBC and CNN. Six months later, Iranian television suggested the incident was a plot in which Āghā-Soltān had faked her own death in front of the cameras, and later been murdered by her fellow conspirators.[8]

Clueless

What all these claims had in common was an insistence that the videos and publicity could not simply be due to grassroots activists with phone cameras and YouTube accounts. People used to controlling information may be angry when their power is bypassed, but their initial reaction is often one of surprise. In both Iran and Britain, they consistently failed to grasp the power that lies in the hands of anyone with an internet connection.

Despite the fallout from the G20 protests, the UK police continued to ignore social media. The next year saw a wave of student protests, triggered by the new government's decision to treble university tuition fees in England as part of its austerity agenda. There were several allegations of police violence. Alfie Meadows, a philosophy student, needed brain surgery after being beaten over the head with a police truncheon. It was Meadows, rather than his attacker, who was taken to court, charged with 'violent disorder'.[9]

There was widespread public shock when one protester, Jody McIntyre, was dragged out of his wheelchair by a police officer. McIntyre says he was removed from his wheelchair twice. The YouTube clip of one of the incidents was enough to trigger anger on the part of people not normally sympathetic to leftwing activists.[10] The BBC's current affairs television programme *Newsnight* provoked thousands of complaints when its interviewer asked McIntyre if he had been 'rolling towards' the police and throwing missiles at them.[11] 'Has it come to this?' asked *The Guardian*'s Kira Cochrane, 'The police dragging a man with cerebral palsy through our streets?'[12]

As time went on, it became apparent that the police were not only underestimating the importance of the internet. Many of them simply did not understand it. This problem went to the highest levels. During the riots of August 2011, Tim Godwin, the acting commissioner of the Metropolitan Police – the London police force – considered asking for Twitter to be 'switched off'.[13] Only after he had raised the possibility was he told that he had no legal authority to do such a thing, even if it were technologically feasible. Furthermore, the rioters turned out to have used BlackBerry Messenger far more than Twitter. The most senior police officer in the UK had revealed that he was utterly clueless about social media.

The Iranian protests of 2009 fizzled out, to the disappointment of both Iranian democracy campaigners and Western governments. Many Western leaders loudly condemned the undemocratic nature of the Iranian government while continuing to defend other brutal regimes in Saudi Arabia, Bahrain and elsewhere.

The *Washington Post*'s description of a 'Twitter revolution' made a big impact on how the Iranian uprising was seen. It is an interpretation that has many critics. Anabelle Sreberny, professor of global media at the University of London, argues that the role of Twitter in the Iranian protests was 'massively overrated'.[14] The Iranian blogger Hamid Tehrani takes a middle line, suggesting that 'Twitter was important in publicizing what was happening, but its role was overemphasized'.[14]

Tehrani's reference to publicity is significant. Twitter ensured that information about events in Iran became widely known. Twitter also played host to exaggerations, rumors and outright lies. It was the use of cellphone cameras and YouTube that allowed people around the world to see the reality of what was going on. In the earlier days of cyberactivism, few people had computers that could play film clips with sound, let alone the technology to film incidents for themselves.

Some notes of caution should be sounded here. Let's remember that the Iranian regime did not fall and that the police officers who attacked Ian Tomlinson and Nicola Fisher were not convicted of any crime. The British journalist Nick Cohen has criticized 'net utopians' who believe that cameraphones will reduce police brutality. He points out that they seem to have made no difference to the vicious police response to protests in Belarus in 2011.[15] He has a point. However, it is difficult to know when cameraphones *have* made a difference. In some countries, at least some police decisions over tactics may have been influenced by fear of filming.

It would be naïve not to recognize that the power of cyberactivism in Iran was affected by the country's hostile relationship with the West. The Iranian regime's reluctance to allow entry to Western journalists left many of them dependent on the internet. Western sympathy with the Iranian resistance movement led to clips that originated on YouTube being shown on mainstream television more than might otherwise have been the case.

The YouTube revolution was not about the power of the internet alone. In many countries the influence of activist films has been enhanced when mainstream journalists have shown them on television. This is a reminder that mainstream media remain at least as important as the internet when it comes to the prospects for grassroots campaigns. To note this is not to deny the reality of grassroots resistance, nor the real threat that cyberactivism poses to the powerful.

In both Iran and Britain, the significance of social media in 2009 lay in its ability to undermine the power of élites to control communication. But as global anger over economic injustice began to boil over, the activist use of social media was about to move onto another stage, in which it would have more effect on the way in which social movements worked as well as the effectiveness of their campaigns. The real Twitter revolution was about to begin.

1 'Police invasion on people, Tehran, Vanak Square,' YouTube, 13 Jun 2009. **2** Paul Mason, *Why It's Kicking Off Everywhere*, Verso, 2012. **3** John Chapman, 'G20 victim: I deserve an apology from the top,' *Daily Express*, 18 Apr 2009. **4** Cited by Mason, *op cit.* **5** Krista Mahr, 'Neda Āghā-Soltān,' *Time*, 8 Dec 2009. **6** Damien McElroy, 'Iran bans prayers for "Angel of Freedom" Neda Agha-Soltan,' *Daily Telegraph*, 22 Jun 2009. **7** Andrew Malcolm, 'Iran ambassador suggests CIA could have killed Neda Agha-Soltan,' *Los Angeles Times*, 25 Jun 2009. **8** 'Neda's death: Other side of the coin,' Press TV, uploaded onto YouTube 6 Jan 2010. **9** 'Jury fails to agree in Alfie Meadows case,' *The Independent*, 19 Apr 2012. **10** 'Jody McIntyre being dragged out of his wheelchair by police,' YouTube, 14 Dec 2010. **11** *Newsnight*, broadcast on BBC2 on 13 Dec 2010. **12** Kira Cochrane, 'Jody McIntyre: "Why is it so surprising that the police dragged me from my wheelchair?",' *Guardian* website, 15 Dec 2010. **13** Mark Hughes and Raf Sanchez, 'London Riots: Met chief Tim Godwin considered shutting off Twitter,' *Daily Telegraph*, 16 Aug 2011. **14** Cited by Evgeny Morozov, *The Net Delusion*, Allen Lane, 2011. **15** Nick Cohen, *You Can't Read this Book*, Fourth Estate, 2012.

3

The hashtag revolution

The Uncut movement against tax-dodging that went viral. The Slutwalks that became a global phenomenon. Two very different forms of protest that took off thanks in part to a simple Twitter device called the hashtag.

On 27 October 2010, about 40 people walked into a Vodafone store in London's Oxford Street, armed only with banners and slogans. The management responded by closing the store. Neither the protesters nor the managers knew that they were making history.

Not long before, a small group of people – mostly friends who had worked together on environmental activism – had met in a London pub to share ideas about how to campaign against the austerity program announced by the UK's new government. Ministers had said they would cut the welfare bill by £7 billion ($11 billion). It had just been reported that Vodafone had done a deal with the revenue to let them off £6 billion ($9.6 billion) of outstanding tax. The protesters called on the government to crack down on corporate tax dodging. This, they said, was an alternative to the cuts. The group called themselves UK Uncut.

Three days later, UK Uncut held a weekend of action. There were 12 protests at stores accused of tax-dodging in various parts of Britain.

When it came to the second weekend of action, only weeks later, the number of protests jumped to 40.[1] People in towns and cities across the UK set up their own autonomous groups: there was Bradford Uncut, Birmingham Uncut, Glasgow Uncut, Belfast Uncut – the list went on and on.

UK Uncut was not the only activist movement taking off in Britain. As the coalition government announced its plan to treble the cap on university tuition fees in England, there was an explosion of student activism that had not been seen for more than two decades. Students occupied their own universities, colleges and even secondary schools throughout England and even, to a lesser extent, in other parts of the UK, where the new fees would not apply. Thousands of students and lecturers marched through London and other cities. As UK Uncut's campaign seeped into the national consciousness, student activists backed calls for a crackdown on corporate tax avoidance as an alternative to increased fees and education cuts. Many of the occupations lasted for several weeks, although most ended or gradually fizzled out after Parliament narrowly voted to approve the new fees on 9 December.[2]

On the Saturday before Christmas 2010, UK Uncut supporters blockaded the flagship branch of Topshop on Oxford Street. The company's owner, Philip Green, had avoided tax by diverting millions of pounds to Monaco. The activists chanted 'Where did all the money go? They sent it off to Monaco!' Protests at branches of two of Green's other companies, Burton Menswear and Dorothy Perkins, led to the stores being closed for the rest of the day.[3]

UK Uncut had succeeded in shutting shops belonging to one of the most powerful billionaires in Britain on the most profitable day of the year. The event was a particular embarrassment for the new Conservative Prime Minister, David Cameron, who had recently appointed Philip Green to advise the government on money-saving and efficiency.[4]

'I don't think anyone involved foresaw how huge UK Uncut

would become,' says Emma Draper, one of the group's first activists. 'It all just kind of happened and seemed to get bigger and bigger.'[5]

The origins of UK Uncut have already become shrouded in legend. The number of individuals who were supposedly present at the original meeting in the pub seems improbably high. There are even conflicting accounts as to which pub it was. What is clear is that a mass movement that shifted political debate began with a small group of anti-cuts activists hitting on a clever idea.

From the beginning, there were those who attributed the movement to the internet. There were others who sneeringly insisted that this was a group of long-standing activists who had earlier campaigned on other issues and would move on to something else soon. In the early days, there were suggestions that they were all simply friends of each other.

It is true that a number of those involved in the first few protests knew each other, either as friends or through campaigning. Many had been involved in the Climate Camp movement. But the number of protests, and the range of people on them, quickly revealed the spontaneous nature of UK Uncut. The media featured stories of pensioners joining UK Uncut protests alongside their grandchildren.

From local to global

Almost four months to the day after the first Vodafone protest in London – on 26 February 2011 – there were 50 protests at sites across the United States. They were mostly at branches of the Bank of America, which had been accused of paying virtually no tax in 2009 or 2010.[6] US Uncut had been born.

Three days later, the 'founding charter' of France Uncut appeared on the internet. It called a day of action on 26 March.[7] The next month, as Canadians approached a general election, supporters of Canada Uncut protested around the country.[8]

Before long, there was Netherlands Uncut, Australia Uncut, Sudan Uncut, Mexico Uncut. Most Uncut groups remained relatively small, with the largest Uncut networks in the UK, France and North America.

How did the Uncut movement spread? Part of the answer lies in the appeal of its message in many countries in which the rich seemed to have caused an economic crisis for which the rest of the population were required to pay. There is nothing unusual about protests in one country triggering protests in others. This has been happening for centuries. What was new was the way in which the structure of UK Uncut allowed it to spread quickly and, in turn, how this movement was helped by the internet.

This time, Twitter really was central to what was going on. Unlike some social media tools, the format of Twitter is fairly simple. Anyone can post a tweet – a message of up to 140 characters – at any time and about anything. A Twitter user can follow any number of fellow users, so that all the tweets of those users appear on their screen. They can also search for a topic that's being discussed and see all the tweets relating to it. They can send messages directly to another user, either privately or so that the conversation is publicly visible. Many tweets are innocuous comments about how someone's day is going or what they're eating for dinner. Some are observations about sport or music. Many express views about politics, religion or current affairs.

From the early days of Twitter, it was clear that it could be used to promote campaigning events. If you want to organize a demonstration, you can tweet about it long in advance, and continue doing so until it is due to happen. If you need to keep it secret, you might want to mention it on Twitter only at the last moment, or to tell your Twitter followers in advance to watch out for a tweet with the details at a particular time. This became a frequent tactic of the Uncut campaigners, although they were not the first to use it.

This way of working can be just as useful for a centrally organized group as for a diverse network of spontaneous activists. It can be used by a top-down organization whose leaders want to send information to their members – although they risk others reading it and replying to their tweets. However, it was a different feature of Twitter that facilitated the non-hierarchical nature of the Uncut movement: the hashtag.

Originally, Twitter hashtags were intended to make it easier to search for particular topics. Someone interested in the transnational oil company BP can type 'BP' into the search box on Twitter. The problem is that it will produce any tweet with those two letters together, including references to other organizations who use them as an acronym. If an environmental activist – or an oil dealer – wants to make clear that BP is the main subject of a tweet, they can write '#BP'. The hashtag indicates the importance of the word that follows it. Someone searching for references to BP can enter '#BP' in the search box and find tweets about the oil trade.

The organizers of the first UK Uncut protests used the hashtag '#UKUncut' on their tweets. This made it easy to search for details about their protests, as well as to join discussions about them. But of course, organizers do not own hashtags. Anyone wanting to organize a UK Uncut action in their own town could tweet about it and write '#UKUncut' at the end of the tweet. Not only had they organized a protest, but with a click of a mouse, they had made themselves part of UK Uncut.

Emma Draper believes that the use of social media allowed the protests to turn into 'a national and then international movement with no real central co-ordinated leadership'. In 2010 and 2011, branches of UK Uncut, US Uncut and other Uncut networks sprang into being whenever anyone used the hashtag, announced an action on Twitter and turned up with others to protest.

Academics call this pattern of working 'networked horizontalism'. Non-hierarchical movements can bring together individuals and groups without some of them having authority over others.

The US activist and trainer George Lakey describes the sort of actions used by the Uncut movement as 'propaganda of the deed'. They make an idea clear and noticeable through physical action. Writing in 1973, Lakey said: 'On a transnational level, there have rarely been experiments with propaganda of the deed, largely because the awareness and organization are only now emerging'.[9] Nearly four decades later, technology has helped transnational direct action to become commonplace.

Shifting the debate

UK Uncut reached a crucial point on 26 March 2011, a date chosen months earlier by the Trades Union Congress for a major anti-cuts demonstration. As thousands of trade unionists marched through London, members of anarchist groups smashed shop windows in Oxford Street and several companies associated with tax avoidance closed their London shops for the day. UK Uncut had promised a major piece of nonviolent direct action during the afternoon, but had said that they would not announce the location until the last moment. As police stood several lines deep around Topshop and Vodafone, UK Uncut declared that they would occupy Fortnum & Mason, a luxury food store in London's Piccadilly. They cited tax avoidance by its parent company, Whittington Investments. Some 145 supporters of UK Uncut made it into the store before police removed customers and staff and surrounded the building. Many other activists gathered outside.

Previously, the police response to UK Uncut had been relatively mild. There had been a number of forced removals but few arrests. Now their tactics changed. All 145 protesters were arrested, locked up overnight and deprived of their clothes and mobile phones. Reports in the rightwing media linked them to the window-breakers and claimed that they had intimidated customers, a claim that was soon undermined by video evidence.[10]

At the same time that British protesters were being arrested in Fortnum & Mason, Uncut actions were taking place throughout France. In March and April, there were similar protests across Canada and the US. UK Uncut actions continued over the following months, although the arrests at Fortnum & Mason deterred some supporters from becoming involved in civil disobedience.

A number of UK Uncut activists became concerned that they were focusing exclusively on corporate tax avoidance rather than on wider issues involving the cuts. Later in the year, they blocked Westminster Bridge – one of the main routes across the River Thames in central London – in protest against the proposed National Health Service Bill, widely seen as an attempt by the government to partly privatize the health service.[11] In 2012, they organized several protests alongside the group Disabled People Against Cuts, including a street party outside the home of Deputy Prime Minister Nick Clegg[12] and a blockade of the Department for Work and Pensions.[13]

Blog sites, Twitter and Facebook all saw discussions about the future of the Uncut movement. There had always been different views within the movement about the balance between a specific focus on tax dodging and a wider approach to fighting cuts. Many were concerned to provide concrete and believable alternatives to cuts to counter government rhetoric about national debt. For some, the success of their message on tax dodging was a reason to keep up the pressure on it. For others, it was grounds for developing their approach further. Peace groups were keen to point out that cutting military spending would make great savings to the national budget. In the UK, the heavy impact of the cuts on disabled people and people in poverty became ever clearer during 2011. Some argued that the priority should be to make more of the public aware of the effect of cuts on people's everyday lives.

Speaking at a conference on web-based activism in June 2012, Danielle Paffard, one of UK Uncut's longstanding activists, expressed concern that the movement was still too associated with tax issues. 'We've been very successful on tax avoidance,' she said. 'But the point of that was to highlight alternatives to the cuts. Even if we stop all tax avoidance completely, if that money's not ploughed back into public services, then it would be easy to see that as a campaign win but actually it would be a loss.'[14]

Despite these concerns, the impact of the Uncut movement has largely been around the issue of wealthy tax dodgers. Its effectiveness in this area is hard to overstate. In a number of countries over the space of a few months, Uncut actions shifted the issue of tax avoidance from a matter of marginal concern to the center of political debate. In doing so, they made it harder for governments in the UK, US and elsewhere to present their cuts as the only way to balance the books. Significantly, they also helped to keep alive the memory that it was the rich who had done most to cause the economic crisis, and the rich who could pay to resolve it.

Tax dodging now seems such an important political issue that it can be easy to forget that until recently it was barely debated at all. Campaigning accountant Richard Murphy, one of the first researchers to work on these issues, can find no reports by any major NGO on international tax avoidance prior to a little-noticed Oxfam report in 2000.[15] In 2003, he and John Christensen set up the Tax Justice Network. Around 2009, the issue was taken up by international NGOs such as Christian Aid and various smaller campaigning groups. The next year, Nicholas Shaxson wrote *Treasure Islands: Tax havens and the men who stole the world*, published in January 2011.[16]

But by far the biggest change came after companies such as Vodafone, Topshop and Boots found themselves peacefully occupied by anti-cuts activists in late 2010 and early 2011. Only then did the web and the mainstream media come alive with discussion of corporate tax avoidance. Richard Murphy argues that the Tax Justice Network laid the ground for UK Uncut, but he readily acknowledges that 'They've done things the Tax Justice Network has not done. The pressure they have brought to bear on UK companies has been enormous. It has also had a real political impact.'[15]

These developments have made many more people aware of the massive amounts lost to public finances when the rich can get away with paying little or no tax. The sums in question are almost impossible to imagine. The Tax Justice Network estimates that funds held in tax havens by individuals total around $11.5 trillion – that's a million dollars multiplied eleven and a half million times. The amount lost to tax revenue as a result is about $250 billion. This is five times what the World Bank estimated in 2002 was needed to address the United Nations' 'Millennium Development Goal' of halving world poverty.[17] Chaminda Jayanetti of False Economy (a group that monitors the cuts in the UK) has compared Britain to a family going hungry because they have vast amounts of food in a cupboard they cannot get into. In the same way, countries are facing heavy cuts while billions of dollars are locked away in economically useless tax havens.[18]

Murphy is keen to stress that campaigning has led to concrete successes. British ministers closed one of the more minor tax loopholes, that allowed companies to avoid purchase tax on online sales by routing them via the Channel Islands. They also ended the UK's subsidy for the Isle of Man, which had helped it to function as a tax haven.

Across the Atlantic, the transnational company General Electric buckled to pressure from US Uncut in April 2012 and promised to return $3.2 billion paid in a 'tax benefit'.[19] The US now requires oil and gas companies to present accounts on a country-by-country basis. According to Christian Aid, this makes it much harder to cover up tax dodging. A similar policy is being debated by the European Union.

The effect of campaigns against tax dodging is not always easy to measure. As Paul Mason put it in 2012, 'There are billions of pounds more going into the exchequer now, because there are companies terrified of being invaded'.[20]

Slutwalking

As Uncut activism was in full swing, a remark by a Canadian police officer triggered a movement that showed that hashtag revolution could lead to very different forms of transnational campaigning. Constable Michael Sanguinetti was speaking at a safety forum in York University in Toronto. In a remark that he has since been given cause to regret, he said: 'I've been told I'm not supposed to say this. However, women should avoid dressing like sluts in order not to be victimized.'[21]

The remark was reported by a student newspaper, *Excalibur*. The paper also quoted a student who had been present at the event, Ronda Bessner, who made an official complaint to the police. She accused the constable of 'blaming the victim'. She added: 'He's also not making victims feel safe to go to the police. It's quite astounding that in 2011 you hear comments like that from a professional.'[21]

Two local feminist campaigners, Heather Jarvis and Sonya Barnett, were so angry that they decided to organize a rally that would march to the Toronto police headquarters. They insisted that Sanguinetti's remark was not unusual. They cited examples of women reporting sexual abuse only to find police joking on their radios about the clothes that the victim was wearing. This latest example of victim-blaming was, in Heather Jarvis' words, 'the final straw'.[22]

'We started planning,' says Jarvis. They began by promoting the event online. 'We put up a Facebook page and a Twitter page and a Wordpress page.' They decided to take this word that Sanguinetti had used and throw it back. They named their event a 'Slutwalk'.

The organizers were contacted by students at York University who were keen to work with them. The rally was never intended to be anything other than a one-off event. As messages of support poured in online, Jarvis said to Barnett, 'Wouldn't it be amazing if 100 people showed up?' Like the founding activists of UK Uncut, they had no idea what was about to happen.

On 3 April 2011, around 4,000 people rallied in Queen's Park in Toronto. They were mostly women, but the group included several hundred men. After listening to speeches, they marched to the city's police headquarters to protest against the victim-blaming attitudes demonstrated by the Toronto police.

Heather Jarvis explains: 'There were survivors [of sexual abuse]. There were allies. There were young people. There were old people. There were feminists. There were sluts. There were parents. There were queers and trans people. There were sex workers. There were people of color and indigenous people. There were families and friends. There were so many people.'[23]

The walk sparked the imagination of millions of women who were angry at being victimized for their choices and blamed for assaults against them. In the following weeks, there were Slutwalks across Canada, and others in the US and New Zealand/Aotearoa.

In June, there were Slutwalks in Mexico City, Matagalpa in Nicaragua and Tegucigalpa in Honduras. In July, they were held in Bhopal and Delhi. On 4 December, there were simultaneous marches in Kuala Lumpur, Singapore and Hong Kong. Within a year of the first Slutwalk in Toronto, there had been Slutwalks in over 250 cities worldwide.[24] In all cases, they were organized by local women.

Jarvis says: 'We always encouraged people to come as they were comfortable, dressed as they were comfortable. And no matter what they were wearing, they deserved respect.' Many participants followed this advice, emphasizing that women of all backgrounds and lifestyles are harmed by victim-blaming. Some chose to dress in clothing considered revealing. They sought to demonstrate their right to dress as they wished without being assaulted, or to enjoy their sexuality without this being seen as 'asking for it'. Placards carried by a number of women in short, low-cut dresses read 'It's a dress, not a yes'. Unsurprisingly, it was this aspect of the movement that sometimes captured the interest of mainstream media. Organizers expressed their frustration at the number of supposedly reputable media outlets that portrayed Slutwalks as consisting entirely of provocatively dressed women. YouTube carried images that told a different story.

For many participants, Slutwalks were empowering and liberating events, breaking down artificial barriers between the personal and political. Selene, a woman marching in Slutwalk London in Britain, told me she was there because she had been raped when she was 13. 'Before today I'd only ever told one person about it,' she explained. She was 27. At Slutwalk she felt able to be open about it for the first time. 'I'm quite active online,' she added, 'with petitions and just raising awareness.' But this was the first time she had joined a march. The Slutwalk movement had taken her activism from the internet to the streets.[25]

As with the Uncut movement, the internet played a central role for Slutwalks. Anyone could plan a Slutwalk in their own town or city by using the hashtag '#slutwalk' on Twitter. Of course, the organization of an event takes more than merely declaring its existence online, but hashtag activism makes it easier for groups all over the world to become part of a network without needing to be part of the same organization as those who founded it.

"The internet has been pivotal for us both in our successes and in our challenges,' says Heather Jarvis. She reports that the internet has led to mixed results when it comes to criticism of the Slutwalk movement. On the one hand, it has made it easier for the movement's opponents to launch personal attacks on organizers, some of whom have received death threats and rape threats. On the other hand, some critics of the movement have used the internet to engage in constructive discussion.

One example is the group Black Women's Blueprint in the US. They wrote to the organizers of Slutwalk Toronto to ask them to consider changes in response to the needs of women of color. They wanted a change of name, suggesting that many women felt they could never reclaim the word 'slut', because of its historical use by white men to denigrate black women. The two groups engaged in dialogue. The name was not changed, and disagreements remain, but Slutwalk Toronto said they were grateful for the dialogue, while Black Women's Blueprint acknowledge that the Slutwalk movement has made progress towards being more inclusive.[26]

There was clearly a range of views on the use of the word 'slut'. Some Slutwalkers said the word was appropriate to draw attention to the attitudes exemplified by victim-blaming police and politicians. Others felt that they were reclaiming a word previously used as an insult, in the way that many gay, bisexual and trans people – as well as some others – call themselves 'queer' and some disabled activists use the word 'crip'. Yolande Robson, a 17-year-old Slutwalker in London, said that the word 'is often used to demonize women for having a healthy sexual appetite. So if you take "slut" and you say "this is who I am" and you reclaim it, it no longer becomes an insult. It becomes a source of pride.'[27] Some polyamorous people – who engage in committed relationships with more than one other person – have for some years been using the term 'ethical slut' to describe themselves.[28]

Some who had problems with the Slutwalk movement's name were nonetheless prepared to be involved. Jackie De Paz, a 19-year-old Mexican-American organizer of Slutwalk Riverside in California, said the word 'has been used to oppress us, to demean us, to dehumanize us, so it really is a difficult word to reclaim. However, I think most of us can agree with the message that Slutwalk is trying to send, that nobody should be raped, regardless of what they're wearing.'[29]

A distinctive feature of the Slutwalks has been the way in which many of them have taken on a local character and focused on local issues. At Slutwalk Rio, women called for the right to breastfeed their children in public. At Slutwalk Seattle, walkers campaigned for legislation to introduce elected civilian review boards for the police. In South Africa, Slutwalkers protest about 'corrective rape', used against lesbians to 'turn' them straight. In India, marchers generally chose not to use the term 'Slutwalk' and adopted the name 'Besharmi Morcha'. Approximate English translations include 'protest of the shameless'.

In parts of Britain, the movement linked up with Muslim women campaigning against the verbal and physical abuse that they sometimes experience for wearing traditional Muslim dress in public. At Slutwalk Birmingham, Muslim women marched in headscarves alongside women in revealing clothes, both declaring that they have a right to dress as they wish without being subjected to abuse or prejudice.

'I do not wear a miniskirt or a burqa in public – but I vigorously defend the right of women to do so without fear of attack,' said Salma Yaqoob, a Muslim feminist and member of Birmingham City Council, who was then leader of the Respect Party. She added: 'Whether it's a little or a lot, no woman should be shamed, blamed or maimed for the clothes she wears.'[30]

It is hard to think of any other activist movement that has spread so quickly across boundaries of race, religion, culture, class and national borders. Many cities saw a second Slutwalk in 2012, as campaigners determined to turn it into an annual event. Only two months after the first Slutwalk took place in Toronto, the US feminist writer Jessica Valenti declared that 'Slutwalks have become the most successful feminist action of the past 20 years'.[31]

Capturing the imagination

It would be a mistake to play down the many differences between the Uncut movement and the Slutwalks. They were not focused on the same issues and their methods were different in many ways. While the web was important for both of them, their use of it was not identical. However, it would be equally wrong to ignore the similarities that may not be obvious on the surface.

These similarities go some way towards explaining why both movements spread so far so fast. The internet played a vital role, but that in itself does not provide an answer. Many more campaigns have used the internet – indeed many have used Twitter hashtags and operated as horizontal networks – without turning into global movements.

First, there is the appeal of the message and its timing. In the UK, many people had been shocked by the extent of the cuts program announced by the new government in 2010. Nonetheless, polls showed that many believed it was the only way to cut the national deficit. Overwhelmingly, this was how ministers sought to justify it. At a key moment, UK Uncut appeared with their message about tax avoidance and undermined the whole narrative. Demonstrations that simply objected to the cuts would not have made the same impact. An alternative had been provided.

This helps to explain the international appeal of the message. The UK was not the only country in which austerity programs were accompanied by tax avoidance by the wealthy. Cracking down on tax dodging has become a key political issue largely because movements such as UK Uncut and US Uncut have presented it as an alternative to austerity.

In a similar way, Slutwalks drew support across the world, because victim-blaming is so common a phenomenon, especially in the context of sexual violence. This casts a rather poor light on the world, in terms of the inequality and sexism common to so many otherwise varied societies. On the other hand, the resonance of the message of resistance shows how many cultures include large numbers of people who are prepared to resist, encouraged by others doing likewise elsewhere.

George Lakey stresses the importance of 'cultural preparation' for social change. A major part of this is 'discrediting the old order' and reducing its legitimacy.[9] The Uncut and Slutwalk movements are striking examples of this, albeit on specific issues.

This relates to the second key factor: coverage in the mainstream media. As we saw in the last chapter, YouTube coverage of police brutality made an impact partly because it was broadcast on television. The Uncut movement did not spread by social media alone. In the UK, newspapers that were critical of the government gave coverage to the message about tax avoidance. Just as importantly, local newspapers covered UK Uncut actions in their own area because they were unusual and therefore newsworthy.

It has been suggested that the Slutwalks have achieved media coverage because they gave newspapers the opportunity to show photographs of women in skimpy clothes. Sadly, there is probably an element of truth in this. Nonetheless, the very association of women's clothing with political activism was in many places unusual enough to be newsworthy. In some countries, such as India, Slutwalks have been hugely controversial and attempts have been made to ban them – some more successful than others.

This is not to say that the Uncut and Slutwalk movements would have had no impact without mainstream media – but it would have been a lesser impact. Around this time, the growing influence of sites such as Twitter was making it hard for journalists to ignore topics that were dominant online. As journalists followed Uncut actions and Slutwalks on Twitter, boundaries between social and traditional media were breaking down.

'Social media breaks down the control and the hierarchy between the mainstream media and the population,' says Emma Draper. 'I think that UK Uncut was one of the first examples.' Nonetheless, had the message and the tactics been less original, it is unlikely that the media coverage would have been as extensive as it was. The movements' gentle forcefulness and creativity captured the public imagination.

This leads on to the third factor: preparation. One of the most striking statistics about the Uncut movement concerns the 145 protesters arrested in Fortnum & Mason in March 2011. Many – but no means all – were students or recent graduates. Adam Ramsey, who works for the student activist network People & Planet, was among those arrested in the store. Not only does he point out that many of the protesters had been involved in People & Planet, he also estimates that around a third of those arrested had at some point attended People & Planet's Summer Gathering, an annual training event for activists.[32] The training includes campaigning skills, use of the internet and media engagement, as well as nonviolent direct action.

Many people in the UK, including many journalists and politicians, have never heard of People & Planet, let alone of its Summer Gathering. Yet behind movements such as UK Uncut lie training events and other forms of preparation that ensure that actions include people with skills and experience that will help them to be effective. This point is consistently overlooked by those commentators who like to attribute activism solely to the internet. A number of Slutwalks have been organized by people with no prior experience of campaigning, though in several cases experienced activists have worked alongside others. Some of the first Besharmi Morcha marches in India were backed by local women's organizations which helped to counter attempts to have the events banned.

Both the Uncut and Slutwalk movements included large numbers of first-time activists with no background in campaigning. This too has been one of their strengths. Their diversity not only includes people of varied ages and genders; it also brings together both the experienced and the inexperienced.

From global to local

The fourth, and perhaps the biggest, similarity between these movements concerns tactics and structure. Both communicated in new and imaginative ways. Both used the internet to spread their messages and to organize their actions. Most important is the way that they connected the local with the global. They used the internet in a way that allowed local groups to stage actions in local ways while being connected to a global network.

The nonviolent physical occupation of tax-dodging stores had a dramatic impact. 'Suddenly, protesters were somewhere they weren't supposed to be,' explained UK Uncut activist Alex Higgins. 'They were not in the predictable place where they are tolerated and regarded as harmless by the authorities.'

He argued: 'If UK Uncut had just consisted of a march on Whitehall, where we listened to a few speakers and went home, nobody would have heard of it. But this time we went somewhere unanticipated. We disrupted something they really value: trade.'[33]

The last point is important. It is worth thinking about Tim Gee's view that there are three types of power and three types of counterpower (as discussed in Chapter 1). By literally putting themselves in the way of commerce as they challenged media and government narratives, UK Uncut were simultaneously exercising physical counterpower, economic counterpower and idea counterpower. It had been a long time since a UK-wide protest movement had systematically employed all three.

On the whole, the Slutwalk movement has not used all these three forms. Nonetheless, it includes physical counterpower as well as idea counterpower. While on one level, a Slutwalk is like any other protest march, on another level it is something else entirely. It is different from most demonstrations because it involves people doing the thing that they are calling for the right to do. Women asserted their right to walk through their own cities dressed as they wish by literally doing just that. This simple, but in some ways shocking, tactic no doubt helped Slutwalks to capture the public imagination.

In both movements, the tactic was easy to replicate. 'It was a tactic that people could use, in their own time, on their own high street,' says Danielle Paffard of UK Uncut.[34] Making an impact did not require vast amounts of time, experience or money. Heather Jarvis points out that the Slutwalk movement's use of the internet not only helped to publicize their cause but made it easier for more people to be involved in organizing Slutwalks. For many – although not all – people, the internet is free or very cheap to use, whereas publishing leaflets and posters would be too expensive for many informal groups.

At the same time, the tactics could be varied to suit local circumstances or preferences. In British towns in which libraries were under threat of closure, Uncutters 'turned' banks into libraries by arriving with piles of books, offering them to customers and, in some cases, simply quietly reading them together in a group. They made the point that libraries would not need to close if banks and other corporations paid their fair share to society. A Quaker conference was taking place in Oxford in England in February 2011, shortly after news broke of tax avoidance by Barclay's Bank. Quaker activists walked down the road from their conference and held a Meeting for Worship in the bank.[35] The action was significant given that Barclay's had been founded by Quakers, originally dedicated to ethical practices. Slutwalk tactics were also developed in response to local issues. On the day of Slutwalk Jakarta, women wore miniskirts in a direct protest against comments made by the city's governor, who blamed a gang rape on the fact that the victim was wearing a miniskirt.[36]

Neither the Uncut movement nor the Slutwalks can be attributed solely, or even primarily, to the internet. Both could have been organized without it. But it is highly unlikely that they would have taken the form they did without the internet. Hashtag activism – 'networked horizontalism' to use the academic language – allows tactics to be replicated around the world while adapting to local conditions. It helps people of varied cultures and circumstances to take an issue with international significance and make a splash in their own country, city or town. As Uncutters in France put it, 'France Uncut is not an organization, but a spontaneous collection of concrete nonviolent actions'.[37]

The Uncut and Slutwalk movements confused mainstream journalists who wanted to know who the 'leaders' were. A lack of hierarchy is disturbing in deeply unequal societies. Fluid movements are a challenge to people used to rigidly structured institutions – including many leftwing parties and trades unions. This helps to explain why some on the traditional Left have been lukewarm in their response to recent activism. As the political commentator Jonathan Bartley points out:

'Movements allow their members to move closer to the center or closer to the periphery, and even to be ambiguous about whether they are actually in or out'.[38]

In many ways, activist tendencies are in tune with wider social trends. Movements are replacing institutions in many areas of life. In Britain for example, less than one per cent of the population belong to political parties, despite the growth in activism.[39] Many British churches have found that average attendance at worship has remained fairly steady for some years, but that formal membership continues to decline.[40] In the age of Twitter and Uncut, membership is about doing, not joining.

Bartley suggests that 'Movements are adaptable and can change far more easily [than institutions]'.[38] Paul Mason links this to activism by arguing that internet-based networks 'can co-ordinate action and choose targets much faster than hierarchical states or corporations can react'.[41] Let's not forget that non-hierarchical networks have been around for a lot longer than the internet. However, the net makes them much easier to get off the ground.

By the middle of 2011, it was clear that the internet was a powerful tool for non-hierarchical social movements keen to shift political debate and change policies. Could it also help to change social systems and bring down governments? The world was about to find out.

---

1 The precise number of actions said to have taken place on each weekend varies slightly in different accounts, both those written at the time and those written since. The figures given here are those stated by Emma Draper when interviewed on 13 June 2012. **2** Heather Sharp, 'Protesters mount their last stand as fees vote nears', BBC News website, 9 Dec 2010. **3** Mark Townsend, 'High street stores hit in day of action over corporate tax avoidance', *The Observer*, 19 Dec 2010. **4** Patrick Wintour and Larry Elliott, 'David Cameron to back Philip Green's plan to improve Whitehall efficiency', *The Guardian*, 11 Oct 2010. **5** Emma Draper, interviewed 13 Jun 2012. All other quotes from Emma Draper in this chapter are from this interview. **6** Matt Kennard, 'BofA targeted by new direct action group', *Financial Times*, 26 Feb 2011. **7** 'Charte Fondatrice', France Uncut website, 1 Mar 2011. **8** Anne Marshall, 'The Uncut movement comes to Canada', *X-Ray*, 10 Mar 2011. **9** George Lakey, *Toward a Living Revolution*, Peace News Press, 2012. **10** Ian Gallagher and George Arbuthnot, '200 arrested as hardcore anarchists fight police', *Daily Mail* website, 27 Mar 2011. **11** Jesse Strauss, 'British health activists occupy London Bridge', *Al Jazeera* English website, 9 Oct 2011. **12** John Fahey, 'Anti-cuts "street party" protest held on Nick Clegg's road', *The Independent*, 26 May 2012. **13** 'Disabled activists and UK Uncut blockade the DWP and Atos' HQ in protest against welfare cuts', UK Uncut website, 31 Aug 2012. **14** Dani Paffard, speaking at the Netroots UK conference, London, 30 June 2012. **15** Richard Murphy, delivering the Beckly Lecture at the British Methodist Conference, Plymouth, UK, 2 Jul 2012. **16** Nicholas Shaxson, *Treasure Islands*, Vintage, 2011. **17** 'Tax havens cause poverty', Tax Justice Network website, accessed 1 Oct 2012. **18** Chaminda Jayanetti, quoted by Symon Hill, 'Mind the gap', *Third Way*, Oct 2011. **19** 'US Uncut welcomes GE's change of heart', US Uncut website 13 Apr 2012. **20** Paul Mason, speaking at the Netroots UK conference, London, 30 June 2012. **21** Quoted by Raymond Kwan, 'Don't dress like a slut: Toronto cop', *Excalibur*, 16 Feb 2011. **22** Heather Jarvis, interviewed 6 Aug 2012. Other quotes from Heather Jarvis in this chapter are from this interview, except when specified. **23** Heather Jarvis, speaking on 'Feminist Magazine', KPFK Radio, 31 Jul 2012. **24** There are varied estimates of the number. This is the figure given by Heather Jarvis when interviewed on 6 Aug 2012. **25** Selene, interviewed at Slutwalk London, 22 Sep 2012. **26** Report and discussion on 'Feminist Magazine', KPFK Radio, 31 Jul 2012. **27** Yolande Robson, interviewed at Slutwalk London, 22 Sep 2012. **28** See Dossie Easton and Janet W Hardy, *The Ethical Slut*, Celestial Arts, 2009. **29** Jackie De Paz, speaking on 'Feminist Magazine', KPFK Radio, 31 Jul 2012. **30** Salma Yaqoob, 'Support the Slutwalk', salmayaqoob. com 17 Jun 2011. **31** Jessica Valenti, 'Slutwalks and the future of feminism', *Washington Post*, 3 Jun 2011. **32** Adam Ramsey, interviewed 22 Aug 2012. **33** Quoted by Johann Hari, 'How to build a progressive tea party', *The Nation*, 3 Feb 2011. **34** Dani Paffard, speaking at the Netroots UK conference, London, 30 Jun 2012. **35** Symon Hill, 'Protest at Barclays', *The Friend*, 25 Feb 2011. **36** 'Indonesian women don miniskirts in rape protest', *Jakarta Globe*, 18 Sep 2011. **37** France Uncut website, accessed 26 Sep 2012. Thanks to Nicola Sleap for translating the text. **38** Jonathan Bartley, *Faith and Politics After Christendom*, Paternoster, 2006. **39** Ali Miraj, 'Introducing the Contrarian Prize', *The Independent*, 17 Sep 2012. **40** For more detail, see Symon Hill, 'The Hashtag Revolution', *Third Way*, Sep 2012. **41** Paul Mason, *Why It's Kicking Off Everywhere*, Pluto Press, 2012.

'We are next!'

Catalyst or tool? What part did the internet play in the cascading revolutions and rebellions that became known as the Arab Spring or Arab Awakening?

'The Tunisian revolution won't spread,' insisted Stephen M Walt, Harvard Professor of International Relations, the day after Tunisia's dictator Zine El Abidine Ben Ali was removed from power. Walt insisted that 'revolutionary cascade is quite rare'.[1]

The Tunisian revolution of 2010-11 came as a surprise to international commentators, politicians and the mainstream media. Despite this, many of them responded by insisting that it was a one-off. A few days later, the US Secretary of State, Hillary Clinton, said 'the Egyptian government is stable,' even as thousands of people were demonstrating in Cairo.[2] Like several other Western leaders, she had good reason to hope that this was the case. The regime of Hosni Mubarak was a key US ally and no amount of internal repression had reduced her enthusiasm for supplying him with weapons.

Both Walt and Clinton were soon proved wrong. Within months, the Tunisian, Egyptian and Libyan dictatorships had been removed, the governments of Bahrain and Syria had unleashed massive violence in order to cling onto power, Israel was rocked by a record level of internal protest and the Saudi regime was looking around nervously.

We are not afraid

If you had asked an international commentator about Tunisia prior to 2010, he or she would probably have told you that it was more prosperous and more stable than other countries in North Africa and less likely than its neighbors to experience social unrest. This view was widespread, commonly accepted, supported by a degree of evidence – and wrong.

In the town of Sidi Bouzid on 17 December 2010, a 26-year-old street vendor called Mohamad Bouazizi set himself on fire after his scales were confiscated by a police officer whom he could not afford to bribe (the details are disputed by the police officer in question). His decision seemed to have been made on the spur of the moment. His family later said that he had been bullied almost every day by police officers.[3] For Bouazizi, this was one humiliation too many.

That night, protests began at the local governor's office. Protesters threw coins at the building, shouting 'Here is your bribe!'.[4] As demonstrations spread across the country, they were violently suppressed by police.

Some early protests concentrated specifically on Bouazizi's treatment. They quickly moved to focus on the issues that had led him to set fire to himself – bribes, jobs, poverty and continuing mistreatment by police and other state officials. Tunisia may have been more affluent than most of Africa, but its wealth was not being shared. The Ben Ali government was focused on attracting transnational corporations and the global economic crisis was making a big impact. By the time the protests began, youth unemployment had reached 30 per cent and inflation was leading to big hikes in food prices.[5] The issue of bribery linked the distresses of everyday life with the thoroughly corrupt nature of the regime. It did not take long for protesters to start chanting against the government itself and demanding political change.

Significantly, the protests were ignored for weeks by Tunisian television. When there is a media blackout on dissent, it can be difficult for protesters in one town even to know about protests in other areas. It can be hard for potential demonstrators to have the courage to turn up if they fear they will be the only ones. There had been isolated demonstrations and even riots in Tunisia in preceding years but they had not spread.

This time, the news got out – and inspired others. Mohamad Bouazizi's cousin, Ali Bouazizi, posted a video online of the first protest. It was noticed by journalists on Al Jazeera, who played it on television within hours.

'We could protest for two years here, but without videos no-one would take any notice of us', explained activist Rochdi Horchani. It was not only videos. Activists communicated via Facebook, despite state surveillance of social media. Tunisia has one of the highest rates of internet access in Africa. At the time of the revolution, a third of the population were online and a quarter had Facebook accounts.[6] Much internet use in the country takes place through mobile phones. Horchani said that he protested on the streets with 'a rock in one hand, a cellphone in the other'.[7]

Aside from Al Jazeera, most international media outlets initially showed little interest. The BBC did not cover the Tunisian protests on its website until more than a week after they began, when the police fired on demonstrators.[8] By 27 December, mass protests had reached the capital, Tunis, and the world began to notice.[9] Protests on similar issues broke out in neighboring Algeria.[10]

The government now realized that they could not simply wait for the protests to go away. Ben Ali tried both to condemn the demonstrators and to pay them off with minimal concessions. He attacked 'hostile elements' who had 'pushed innocent students to commit acts of disorder, violence and anarchy'. But he also visited Mohamad Bouazizi in hospital and announced changes to tax rules.[11]

It was too late. By now, nationwide protests had given the people too much confidence to be bought off with questionable promises. On 4 January, after 18 days in hospital, Mohamad Bouazizi died from his burns. Tunisia had already seen the sacrifice of others who had set themselves on fire, and one man who had electrocuted himself on top of a pylon as he protested about unemployment.[12] A few days later, the International Federation of Human Rights in Paris estimated that 50 Tunisian protesters had been killed by police. Striking factory workers were joined by striking teachers and lawyers. Most protesters continued to avoid violence, although in some cases they resorted to throwing rocks and Molotov cocktails and burning vehicles. As protesters struggled with police in the working-class Ettadem neighborhood of Tunis, they chanted, 'We are not afraid! We are not afraid!'[13]

Ben Ali responded by announcing a plan to create 300,000 new jobs.[11] It made no difference. Even he realized the game was up. On 14 January, four weeks to the day since Mohamad Bouazizi had set himself on fire, Zine El Abidine Ben Ali fled Tunisia. The French government, a longstanding ally of his regime, refused to allow his plane to land on French soil. He was given shelter in Saudi Arabia.[14]

As Tunisians celebrated, an attempt at a unity government collapsed within days after trade unionist members objected to the inclusion of ministers from Ben Ali's RCD party. Protesters returned to the streets. On 23 October, Tunisians voted in their first post-revolution election. Ennhada, a relatively moderate Islamist party, took 41 per cent of the vote and formed a coalition with secular center-left groups.

Building counterpower

The term 'Arab Spring' became common as protests spread across North Africa and the Middle East in early 2011. Some, who see it as a longer process, prefer to call it the 'Arab Awakening'. When did it begin? Conventional wisdom cites

Bouazizi's sacrificial protest as the starting-point. In contrast, veteran US activist Noam Chomsky points to the Gdeim Izik protest camp, set up by campaigners in Western Sahara on 9 October 2010.[15] We could go back further, to the launch of the 'April 6 Youth Movement' in Egypt in 2008, or we could rewind several decades to the fallout from the Second World War and the independence movements that followed it. While mass media coverage tends to focus only on recent and unusual events, the background to most social changes can be traced back for years, if not centuries. In Egypt, resistance to the regime had been steadily building for over a decade before it fell, not always in ways that attracted international attention. Several, but by no means all, of those ways involved the internet.

Egypt's president Hosni Mubarak had ruled the country since 1982, suppressing Islamists, liberals and socialists alike. His support for the US and Israel made him as unpopular in his own country as he was elsewhere in the region. Despite his opposition to Islamism, he was not averse to taking advantage of prejudice against the country's Christian minority when he needed a scapegoat.

The most heartfelt oppression was economic. Over the preceding decade, Mubarak's government had slashed public spending and done deals with transnational corporations as a condition for receiving loans. Youth unemployment and food price inflation had reached similar levels as in Tunisia. The economic crash of 2008 came just as demographic and social changes were leading to a much younger population and higher numbers attending university. This led, to use Paul Mason's term, to a large number of 'graduates with no future'. At the same time, conditions in the slums deteriorated. In 2009, the government used the international swine flu epidemic as an excuse to slaughter all the pigs belonging to the *zabbaleen*, Christian slum dwellers who made a living by collecting rubbish and who used their pigs to eat rotten food. The slaughter allowed Mubarak to give a contract to a corporation to collect rubbish instead.[5] By 2010, the national minimum wage stood at the same rate as in 1984.[16]

International observers had been surprised by the Tunisian uprising. They should really have been less surprised by Egypt. The revolution had been building for at least a decade. Tim Gee argues that the first stage of social change is 'consciousness', when increasing numbers of people become aware of the need for change and begin to create 'the conditions for counterpower'.[4] Latin American activists use the term *conscientizacion*. This equates roughly to George Lakey's term 'cultural preparation'. As Lakey puts it, 'People get ready for revolution by changing the way they look at themselves. Private problems become political issues as the people develop a collective will and an understanding of struggle.'[17]

Gee says that in the case of Egypt, 'the consciousness stage of the revolution can be traced back to the year 2000'.[4] Lakey, who has spent years working with underground activists in Egypt and elsewhere, says that it was in 2000 that opponents of the regime from various groups really began to work together.[18] In September of that year, thousands of Egyptians took to the streets to protest against Israeli abuses of human rights in the Occupied Palestinian Territories. By implication, they were also attacking their own government's support for Israel and the US. Two years later, pro-Palestinian protests took off around Cairo University. Hossam el-Hamalawy, an Egyptian socialist who later became a prominent figure in the revolution, said that the 2002 protests were 'the first time I heard protesters *en masse* chanting against the president'.[19]

As el-Hamalawy puts it, they had to 'pull down the wall of fear brick by brick'.[19] The next year, when the US and UK governments invaded Iraq, Egyptian police fired water cannon on a angry crowd of around 10,000 people protesting against the invasion.[20] Later, protesters briefly took over Tahrir Square – 'Liberation Square' in Arabic – in central Cairo and burnt a billboard with Mubarak's picture on it.

It was around this time that activists' use of the internet became more prominent. The launch of the *Kefaya* ('enough') movement combined anti-war and pro-Palestinian concerns and posed an explicit challenge to Mubarak's rule. El-Hamalawy says that Kefaya's 'use of both social and mainstream media helped shift the political culture'. But he admits that it 'failed to create a mass following among the working class and the urban poor'. [19]

The class dynamics began to change in 2006 when Egypt experienced its first major strike for decades. As Mubarak sold off state-owned factories to private companies, a textile mill in the town of Mahalla laid off over a quarter of its staff. Thousands of its workers, mostly women, went on strike in response. They triggered a wave of industrial action across the textile sector. Two years later, on 6 April 2008, the police responded to a protest over food prices in Mahalla by killing at least three people and arresting and torturing hundreds of others.

The protest, which became known as the Mahalla Intifada, led a civil engineer called Ahmed Maher to set up a Facebook page that gained 70,000 members. This was the beginning of the 'April 6 Youth Movement'. Those who paid close attention to developments debated the role of Facebook and other websites in the movement's development.

By 2010, strikes and demonstrations had become relatively frequent. In June of that year, a man called Khaled Said was dragged from an internet café by police officers and killed. He had previously posted a film on YouTube about police corruption. Under Mubarak, such incidents could pass with little comment. This time, critics of the regime set up a Facebook group called 'We are all Khaled Said'. Its co-founder was an employee of Google called Wael Ghonim. He was able to use his technical knowledge to make his identity difficult for the police to trace online. He posted on the page: 'Today they killed Khaled. If I don't act for his sake, tomorrow they will kill me.' [21] Within weeks, 130,000 people had signed up to the page.[22]

Looking back at this, it would be easy to see the outbreak of revolution in 2011 as the obvious consequence of a build-up of resistance. This would be simplistic. A list of the protests and cyberactivism between 2000 and 2010 cannot record the emotions and traumas of activists who at times were beaten back or gave up hope as their comrades were killed by Mubarak's thugs. There are many cases of a country seeing years of increasing protests without the regime falling.

Nonetheless, it is surprising that so few people outside Egypt saw it coming. It is a sign of how much political and media establishments in many countries are wedded to the status quo and can't imagine a major change. As Paul Mason puts it, 'the world's collective imagination failed'.[5]

Shaking in their boots

As Ben Ali fled Tunisia, protesters in Egypt chanted 'We are next! We are next! Ben Ali, tell Mubarak he is next!'.[23] *The Independent*'s Robert Fisk, a veteran commentator on the region, wrote that 'dictators... are shaking in their boots across the Middle East'. But he predicted that Western governments would ensure that dictatorships remained in place.[24] The evidence seemed to back him up. Hillary Clinton, asked about Tunisia only the day before Ben Ali's fall, replied 'We can't take sides'.[23]

Many in the region clearly did not need her support. By the time Ben Ali flew to Riyadh, there were already protests in Algeria, Lebanon and Jordan. Within days they were joined by Egypt, Mauritania, Oman and Saudi Arabia. In several countries, including Algeria, Egypt and Iraq, several people set themselves on fire in public protests over poverty, employment and housing.

Egyptians may have spent a decade building for revolution, but it was Tunisia that sent the spark to ignite it. 'When they saw what happened in Tunisia, the [Egyptian] people realized that there was an Arab people that revolted and demanded its rights,' said Asmaa Mahfouz, a 26-year-old Egyptian activist. 'Following these events, we began to tell people that we must take action, that we must revolt and demand *our* rights.'[25]

Within four days of the fall of Ben Ali, at least four Egyptians had set fire to themselves in anti-government protests. At least one had died. By mid-January, 473,000 people had signed up to the 'We are all Khaled Said' page on Facebook.[22]

Activists designated 25 January as the day for a major protest in Cairo's Tahrir Square. The date was a national holiday as 'Police Day'. It was also the anniversary of an anti-government protest the previous year. A week before the set date, Asmaa Mahfouz wrote on Facebook: 'I'm going to Tahrir Square today'. She said she was too angry to wait another week. She held up a placard in the square and talked about corruption, attracting a crowd who filmed her on mobile phones before the arrival of hundreds of security agents and police. She later posted a film on YouTube. On camera, she said, 'I'm making this video to give you a simple message: we're going to Tahrir on 25 January'.[25]

Police officers can read social media as easily as activists. The campaigners listed fake starting-points on Facebook as a diversion, while meeting up in small groups to approach the square from different directions. Activists in the slums shouted slogans about the price of food and urged others to join them in marching to Tahrir. The police responded with water cannon and teargas. Activists took control of the square, holding spontaneous meetings and communicating with media from around the world. The government tried switching off Twitter across the country. It took activists only four hours to find their way back onto it.[5]

That evening, the Tahrir protesters met to talk about their demands. Some seasoned activists, thinking that things should be taken in stages, suggested calling for the arrest of the Minister of the Interior. Socialist campaigner and blogger Gigi Ibrahim explained: 'But the people around us in Tahrir Square, the majority, who didn't belong to any political group, were chanting for the removal of the regime. So we knew at that moment that we couldn't ask for less than the people wanted'.[26]

On Friday 28 January, Mubarak sacked his entire cabinet. Like Ben Ali before him, the attempt at minor change came too late. The day went down in history as the 'day of rage'. The police escalated their brutality. Several hundred activists are thought to have been killed. Amidst teargas and water cannon, about 4,000 protesters struggled for control of the Qasr al-Nil bridge, which goes over the Nile from Tahrir Square.

As protests continued over subsequent days, Mubarak changed tack. Protesters were attacked by gangs of pro-government thugs. Hand-to-hand fighting led to casualties on both sides, but the pro-Mubarak side were outnumbered. It emerged that many of them were police officers in plain clothes. Protesters found yet another use for the internet when they captured them, removed their police identity cards and displayed them online. Others admitted that they had been paid to attend.

Twitter, not only in Egypt but around the world, was alive with discussion of events in Tahrir Square. On 8 February, Wael Ghonim appeared on television after 12 days of imprisonment and interrogation. As he cried, he insisted 'I am no traitor' and 'I love my country'. He added, 'The heroes are the ones who were on the streets. The heroes are the ones that got beaten up. The heroes are the ones shot and arrested and [who] put their lives in danger. I am no hero.' The enthusiastic response on Twitter made clear that many people disagreed with his final words.[26]

The next day saw demonstrations accompanied by strikes. Trades unions collectively stated that there would be a general strike if Mubarak did not give up power. On 11 February, less than a month after the fall of Ben Ali, Hosni Mubarak resigned.

'I can't stop crying. I've never been more proud in my life,' tweeted Gigi Ibrahim, amidst scenes of celebration in Tahrir Square. 'When we declared our demands ppl [people] thought we were mad,' wrote a Twitter user called Monasosh, 'Look where madness got us.'[27]

Walking like an Egyptian

While protests were under way in Egypt, the world's media talked about another uprising organized on the internet. The Bahraini government responded by rounding up anti-government bloggers. Activists in the country called for a day of protest on 14 February. Mubarak's fall encouraged the protesters, who continued to demonstrate over the following days. After police opened fire on demonstrators, thousands marched in the capital Manama and occupied the Pearl Roundabout, setting up a protest camp. The government poured a massive military presence into the city, using tanks in an attempt to restrict movement and limit demonstrations. But mass protests continued, with the largest involving 300,000 people. Pro-government demonstrations began in response.

The Saudi government, a key ally of the Bahraini regime, sent around 1,000 troops into Bahrain to help to suppress the protests. Troops stormed Pearl Roundabout, where protesters had camped for several weeks, violently removing them. Medical workers who had treated protesters were arrested and beaten. Transnational corporations colluded in the mass firing of workers known for anti-government opinions.[28] But still the protests did not stop. They flared up periodically throughout 2011 and 2012.

The viciousness of the Bahraini authorities was met with a remarkable number of actively nonviolent demonstrations. Elsewhere, activists used violence in the face of repression. Protesters in Libya took control of the country's second-largest city, Benghazi, in February 2011. As the Qadafi regime unleashed massive violence on rebel-supporting areas, opponents of the regime formed an anti-government army. It included people who had defected from the top ranks of Qadafi's government and armed forces. The US and UK – which had been selling weapons to the Libyan regime until a matter of months earlier – declared their support for change and bombed Qadafi's troops.[29] Qadafi was killed in October as anti-government forces took control of Libya. A similar situation emerged in Syria, where thousands of demonstrators protested peacefully before massive military attacks by the regime's forces. Parts of the resistance movement formed the Free Syrian Army. By 2012, civil war was under way in Syria.

Elsewhere, protests led to limited reform. Even before Mubarak fell, the King of Jordan responded to demonstrations by sacking his prime minister. In Algeria, thousands defied the law to protest against both poverty and the lack of democracy. The government lifted a 'state of emergency' that had been in place for 19 years, leading to a limited increase in political freedoms. The Yemeni President, Ali Abdullah Saleh, resigned in the wake of mass protests but left the political system in place and seemed to be exercising influence through his successor. A new level of protest in Saudi Arabia led King Abdullah to announce that women would be able to vote from 2015.[30] The King of Morocco introduced democratic reforms but activists continued to campaign for further change. Months of protests in Kuwait reached a critical point with the occupation of the National Assembly building in November, following which the Emir sacked his government. Smaller-scale protests in Djibouti, Iraq, Mauritania and the Occupied Palestinian Territories led to little immediate change but confirmed that nowhere was immune from the effects of the Arab Awakening.

The repercussions of the awakening were felt across the world. Complicity with dictatorial regimes shot up the news agenda in a number of Western countries. There was embarrassment for David Cameron in the UK over his government's sale of arms to undemocratic regimes including Bahrain, Egypt and Libya.[31] Saudi Arabia is a leading recipient of British weapons. When the Bahraini regime asked for military help from the Saudis, television viewers watched Saudi armored vehicles made in the north of England rolling into Bahrain to crush peaceful protest.[32] UK ministers withdrew arms export licenses for Bahrain, though not Saudi Arabia. Six months later, there were protests in Britain when the government invited the Bahraini regime to send representatives to the London arms fair.[33]

The protesters in Tunis and Tahrir Square were cited as an inspiration for people working for political change, from South Africa to Russia. In May 2011, Spanish campaigners known as the Indignados ('indignant ones') began camping in public squares in protest against austerity policies. Later in the year, the 'Occupy' movement began in the US and spread around the world. Many Indignados and occupiers said they had been inspired by the Arab Spring. We will look at these movements in more detail in the next chapter.

There is one country in the Middle East that is often left out of discussions of the Arab Awakening: Israel.

The country's Prime Minister, Benjamin Netanyahu, had often boasted that Israel was the 'only democracy in the Middle East'. The phrase is used often (to say the least) by supporters of the Israeli government. But Netanyahu did not seem keen on being joined by any other democracies. Egypt's government had been relatively friendly towards Israel and he didn't want that being changed by the Egyptian people. Netanyahu condemned the Arab Spring as 'anti-Western, anti-liberal, anti-Israeli and anti-democratic'.[34] In April 2011, he said 'The world is shaking, but there are no tremors or protests in Israel'.[35]

He didn't have long before his words came back to haunt him. On 14 July, a 25-year-old Israeli graduate called Daphni Leef pitched a tent in the Rothschild Boulevard, an affluent area of Tel Aviv, to protest against high rents and house prices. On Facebook, she invited people to join her. Within weeks, thousands of people were camping out across Israel. It became known as the July 14 movement, or #j14 on Twitter. It was Facebook, rather than Twitter, that seemed to be the dominant organizing tool, although there were numerous discussions and debates at the camps themselves. An opinion poll by the newspaper *Haaretz* found that 87 per cent of Israelis sympathized with the protests.[36]

With much of the movement arising spontaneously on Facebook, there was confusion as to the activists' aims. Some insisted that they were 'apolitical'. The word is as unhelpful as it is bizarre. The cost of housing is an inherently political issue. Some were trying to imply that they had no ideological agenda. They also sought to distance themselves from those Israelis who campaign against the Israeli occupation of the Palestinian Territories. Amidst this confusion, the protest was attacked from both the right and the left. Politicians from the rightwing Likud party called it a 'far-left conspiracy'.[37] Leftwing radicals accused the protest organizers of ignoring Palestinian questions.

Then things began to change. Some protesters were happy to express their enthusiasm for the Arab Spring. YouTube videos of protests elsewhere in the Middle East and North Africa were shared among Israeli activists. There were people marching with placards that read 'walk like an Egyptian'.[38] A large tent appeared at Rothschild Boulevard whose occupants included both Jewish and Palestinian citizens of Israel. They designated it as a place for dialogue and solidarity. When the council elected by protests camps around Israel published a list of demands, they included two points concerning the rights and interests of Palestinians living within Israel. Such Palestinians make up 20 per cent of Israel's population (within the country's official borders; not including the Occupied Territories). Palestinian activist Odeh Bisharat was applauded at one of the movement's largest rallies as he spoke of the injustices experienced by his community. There were chants of 'Jews and Arabs refuse to be enemies!'[39]

On 3 September, Israel experienced the biggest protest ever to take place within its own borders. Around 430,000 people demonstrated over the cost of living, including 300,000 in Tel Aviv and 50,000 in Jerusalem.[38] They chanted, 'The people demand social justice!'

The movement seemed to slowly peter out over the following months. When Netanyahu talked up the possibility of a military conflict with Iran in early 2012, some suggested that he was distracting attention from problems closer to home. As Israeli cyberactivist Ronny Edry put it, 'Nobody's going to talk about the price of milk when we have a war coming'.[40] But when it came to the first anniversary of the protests, there was a revival of activism. Many turned up on 14 July 2012 to raise the same issues of housing and food prices. In a sign of the Arab Spring's ongoing influence, one protester set himself on fire.[41]

The long-term effects of the Israeli protests are very difficult to predict. As with other protests and uprisings in the area, resistance often took the form of non-hierarchical movements whose horizontal structures reflected the 'hashtag activism' discussed in the last chapter. This can have unexpected consequences. Israeli journalist Dimi Reider has made an intriguing suggestion:

> *'On the most practical level, if the protesters had begun by blaming all of Israel's social and political woes on the occupation, none of the breathtaking events of the past three weeks would have happened... Altruist causes can rarely raise people to a sustained and genuine popular struggle against their own governments... But one of the many unexpected consequences of this movement – indeed, the movement itself is an avalanche of completely unexpected consequences – is that these boundaries are beginning to blur and to seem less relevant than what brings people together. We have failed to end the occupation by confronting it head on, but the boundary-breaking, de-segregating movement could, conceivably, undermine it.'[39]*

Revolution by internet?

Books much longer than this one have already been published about the causes of the Arab Awakening. Many more will no doubt be written. This is not the place for an in-depth analysis of its causes. What we can do is to note the ways in which it has been reported and to ask some key questions. In particular, why have the international media focused so much on the role of the internet? And are they right?

From the early days of the Arab Spring, the term 'Twitter revolution', previously used in relation to the Iranian and Moldovan uprisings in 2009, appeared regularly. This was all the more so once the Western media started to pay attention to what was going on. Ben Ali had still not fallen from power when George Brock, Head of Journalism at City University in London, argued that 'This *has* been a social media revolt'.[42] As protests took off in Tel Aviv, Israeli academic Carlo Strenger described it as 'another Facebook revolution'.[37]

Predictably, there was a backlash. Viktor Mayer-Schonberger of the Oxford Internet Institute argued that 'we should be very skeptical' about claims that social media had been central in Tunisia.[43] Evgeny Morozov, who has made a career out of challenging the notion that the internet is helpful for social change, insisted that 'the contribution the internet made was minor'.[44]

The danger with this debate is that we allow ourselves to become entangled between two ridiculous arguments. On the one hand are those who talk as if the internet is the only explanation necessary, ignoring economic causes of unrest or the long-term build-up of resistance. On the other side are those who are so dismissive of technology that they are unwilling to accept that the presence of the internet can have made any impact at all. It is both sad and frustrating that some of the academics and journalists who engage in these debates do not seem to be very interested in hearing the views of people who personally took part in the uprisings.

A more nuanced approach would recognize that the role and importance of the internet varied considerably at different times and in different places. Facebook opened an Arabic-language service in 2009; it had nine million users by 2011. Across the region, internet access increased from 33 to 48 per cent in the three years before the Arab Spring.[5] But we should be careful. For one thing, rates of internet access vary quite considerably across the Middle East and North Africa.

Opinions about social media are of course varied amongst the activists themselves. Bechi Blagui of the Free Tunisia website said 'there is only one name that does justice to what is happening in the homeland: social media revolution'.[45] But Gigi Ibrahim, whose tweets and interviews during the Tahrir Square protests drew worldwide attention, insisted that it was 'just bogus' to talk about a Facebook revolution, although she was speaking in the context of Western media reports on Egypt. She explained: 'We use the internet to communicate and spread information, but if the struggle wasn't there, if the people didn't take to the streets, if the factories didn't shut down, if workers didn't go on strike, none of this would have happened.'[46]

In contrast, Wael Ghonim has used the term 'internet revolution', spoken about the importance of Facebook and called the uprisings 'Revolution 2.0'. While he attributes more to the internet than Ibrahim does, he nonetheless says that the purpose of his cyberactivism was to persuade people 'to take the action onto the street'.[21]

Undoubtedly, the tweets sent from Tahrir Square gave a more immediate and vivid picture of unfolding events than the slower and more detached newspaper and television reports. In Tunisia, the state media's decision to ignore the protests meant that many Tunisians knew what was going on because of the internet. Activists' videos of protests were shared on Facebook. Al Jazeera's Yasmine Ryan reported that 'Most Tunisians did not dare repost the videos on Facebook or even to "like" them... [but] were able to follow news of the uprising on social media thanks to a solid core of activists'.[47]

As we have seen, film clips of the first protests were shown on Al Jazeera, beaming the news to people who would not have come across it on Facebook. This is another example of how the effectiveness of social media is related to its ability to convey a story to mainstream media. The BBC and much of the US-based media paid little attention to the story in its first two weeks, while in French media it was more prominent, affecting levels of awareness in different parts of the world. Rather than attributing the Arab Spring to the internet, or dismissing the net's role altogether, it is far more useful to think about the ways in which it affected the forms that resistance took. For example, as we saw in the last chapter, use of the internet tends to work against hierarchical structures and encourages movements that are more fluid and open-ended. Of course, there is not a straightforward correlation: hierarchical groups can use the internet and there were many non-hierarchical movements long before computers were invented. Nonetheless, relatively high levels of internet use in countries such as Tunisia, Egypt and Israel aided relatively open discussion among opponents of regimes that were falling and discouraged the formation of rigid and top-down organizations.

Non-hierarchical movements are less likely to resort to violence. It is almost impossible for a violent movement to avoid hierarchy for a sustained period of time. Armies are by their nature hierarchical. The majority of protests during the Arab Spring were nonviolent. For many, such as some in Tahrir Square, this was an ethical decision. Some have cited the writings of Gene Sharp, famous practitioner of active nonviolence, although their influence on most protesters in the region has probably been overstated. Nonetheless, millions of people in the region demonstrated what the Indian independence activist Mohandas Gandhi called the 'nonviolence of the strong'. This is not simply about avoiding violence through cowardice or passivity. It is the attitude of those who are brave enough to resist injustice with violence but choose nonviolence instead. Those who refuse to move, who stand in the way, resist power physically but not violently. This often means finding creative ways to resist oppression in particular contexts. In 2012, Palestinian prisoners who were detained without charge in Israeli jails began one of the biggest mass hunger strikes in modern times.[48] Saudi women tried to register to vote or to receive driving licenses, although they were denied the right to do either.[49]

It is possible to support active nonviolence without condemning those who resort to violent resistance in extreme situations. Outside of the region, supporters of the Egyptian and Tunisian uprisings were divided on the use of violence by the opposition in Libya and Syria. While some were clearly turning to weapons in desperation, others took advantage of the civil war for their own ends, such as former members of the Qadafi regime who changed sides. They were hardly opponents of tyranny and violent repression.

Money and power

A central danger of the media focus on the internet is that it overlooks economic causes. As we saw in Chapter 1, the economic crisis of 2008, and the US response of 'quantitative easing', led to a hike in food prices in North Africa and the Middle East.

Issues such as food, bribery and inequality expose the links between money and power. Protests as far apart as Bahrain and Algeria moved rapidly from chanting slogans about prices to calling for the overthrow of governments and changes in political systems. As Lebanese activist Rami Zurayk puts it: 'We are not bellies waiting to be fed. We are human beings seeking freedom'.[50]

All but the wealthy were affected by the economic crisis. These were not protests confined to the very poor. Nor were they the preserve of middle-class intellectuals – however some of them might have been presented by parts of the media. In both Tunisia and Egypt, the revolt stepped up a gear when trades unions came on board and strikes were called. People were resisting the regime economically as well as physically and with ideas. Egyptian trade unionist Kamal Abbas argues that the mass participation of the organized working class made victory 'inevitable'.[25]

Protesters in Tahrir Square included both slum residents and unemployed graduates with laptops. As George Lakey says, 'closer attention to the Egyptian story underlines the cross-class character of the movement in overthrowing Hosni Mubarak: working-class and middle-class people working together'.[17] The sociologist Betsy Leondar-Wright has analyzed activist movements in terms of class support. She reports that success is far more likely in cross-class movements.[51]

Similarly, the resistance movement in Egypt bridged religious divisions. On several occasions in Tahrir Square, Christians formed a protective circle around Muslim protesters so that they could pray without being attacked by the police. The Muslims returned the favor so that the Christian protesters could pray. The pictures inspired religious activists – and others – around the world.

One of the more persistent untruths about the Arab Spring is that the protests were led by Islamist militants. In most cases, Islamist groups joined in only once the protests were under way. In some cases, their members became involved despite their leaders' reluctance. As the British Muslim writer Tariq Ramadan puts it in one of the first major books on the uprisings: 'The Arab Awakening has clearly not been the work of Islamist movements. Neither in Tunisia or Egypt, nor in Jordan, Libya or Syria were they the initiators. The mass movements took to the streets without them, against the will of their leaders and, in any event, without their agreement.'[52]

There were dire warnings from conservative commentators in the West, who suggested that the protests would lead to fundamentalist regimes that would be far worse than Mubarak and Ben Ali. Citing no evidence at all, Melanie Phillips suggested that most Egyptians harbor Islamist and 'anti-Jewish' sentiments – implying that it was therefore best for them not to have democracy.[53] A number of Christian groups and publications in the West expressed fear for the fate of Egypt's Coptic Christian minority when Mubarak fell from power.

It is difficult to know how these people failed to notice the presence of Egyptian Christians in the anti-Mubarak movement. Tariq Ramadan points to the 'presence of non-religious people and secularists [at protests] in Tunisia and Egypt, as well as the highly visible Coptic minority presence on Tahrir Square'.[52] Certain attitudes say more about Western fears than they do about the protesters' religious views.

This is not to deny that Islamist groups have been among the beneficiaries of the Arab Spring. Relatively moderate Islamists have achieved electoral success in Egypt and Tunisia. This has caused very real concern on the part of religious and sexual minorities. Some said that they had been empowered by the movement even though the immediate results were not what they had hoped for. Egyptian feminist Dima Khatib bemoaned the fact that only two per cent of members of the post-Mubarak parliament were women. She said 'we have a long road ahead'. But she also expressed her frustration with Western commentators who used such facts to present prejudiced caricatures of Arabic and Muslim attitudes to gender. She insisted that 'we, Arab women, are not weak... and the Arab revolutions have proved to us that we are stronger than ever we thought'.[54]

A tool, not a cause

The mainstream media's concentration on the role of the internet may seem to be a complete reversal of their position a few years previously. The internet was once dismissed by most of the mainstream media (as we saw in Chapter 1). Now things seem to have swung to the opposite extreme, with social media lauded for its liberating potential. These two approaches are not as dissimilar as they appear. As John Naughton – a champion of the internet long before it became widespread – puts it:

> 'There is an intriguing parallel between the failure of the Tunisian regime to spot the significance of social networking and mainstream media's conviction about its overriding importance. Both camps persist in regarding this stuff as exotic, which for them it is, which in turn highlights how out of touch they have become with reality. For the reality is that the net and social

> *networking have become mainstream, even in societies that seem*
> *relatively underdeveloped to Western eyes... So when significant*
> *things happen – riots, strikes, elections, conflicts and social*
> *upheavals of all kinds – it's only to be expected that they will*
> *use the communication tools with which they are familiar. The*
> *message for dictators, elected politicians and newspaper editors*
> *alike is simple. This is the way things are: get used to it.*[55]

Mainstream media are used to reporting on the actions of the powerful. The rest of us only really get a look in if we do something spectacular, either individually or collectively. A revolution is noticed; a single protest is often not. The steady build-up of counterpower in Egypt went unnoticed by most, including some who were supposed to be experts. When anger exploded onto the streets, those who were taken by surprise needed an explanation and for some (but by no means all) journalists, Facebook and Twitter provided it. Certainly this is more straightforward, and less challenging to an establishment worldview, than recognizing that change had been brewing for years from the ground up.

In the light of this, it is intriguing to reflect on the protests that took place in Saudi Arabia. By the standards of the Arab Spring, the Saudi protests were small indeed. By the standards of Saudi Arabia, they were huge. Under one of the most repressive regimes in the world, there were demonstrations over workers' rights, women's rights, political imprisonment and anti-Shi'a discrimination. Women organized a suffrage campaign on Facebook.[56] Dozens of women drove cars in defiance of the ban on female driving.[57] Several protesters were shot dead by police, others were arrested and tortured and the organizer of online calls for a mass protest was killed shortly before the event could take place.[58]

The numbers involved were small – perhaps comparable to the numbers involved in Egyptian demonstrations in 2000 and 2002. If the Saudi regime is overthrown 10 or 20 years after the fall of Mubarak, will commentators and editors see it as another event that has come out of nowhere and look around for a simple explanation? If counterpower movements build in Saudi Arabia, they will need an incredible degree of courage. They will need to work together and learn the skills of resistance. Whatever use of social media they make, they will probably have spent some time getting used to it.

Nonetheless, the very existence of social media makes it more likely that residents of Saudi Arabia will have access to the knowledge that inspires them, as they read and hear about resistance elsewhere in the region. It makes it easier for Shi'a protesters in the east of the country to liaise with student demonstrators and women's rights activists in Riyadh.

Social media is a tool rather than a cause of social change. Facebook and Twitter did not overthrow Ben Ali or Mubarak, any more than the printing press overthrew Charles I. But they made it easier for the people who did overthrow them to know what was going on. They aided communication and debate between opponents of the regime. Their existence meant that those turning up to a public protest could be confident that they were not alone.

When the House of Saud finally falls, social media will not be the cause. Economic injustice, sexism, political repression and religious discrimination will all have greater claims. But by freeing up communication in this rigidly regulated society, social media may well hasten the day. The same commentators who were surprised by Tahrir Square are now analyzing the Arab Awakening without referring to Saudi Arabia. Perhaps they will get another surprise. In the words of the writer Anthony McRoy:

> *'Given the existence of Al Jazeera, and the social media in general, can it [the Saudi regime] cocoon itself for long with a mixture of Wahhabi rhetoric and economic bribes, or will its cards be finally trumped?... If the region's largest oil-producing*

state, with the added religious prestige of Mecca and Medina, falls to a democratic revolution, where does that leave Western policy in the region, other than in the dustbin of history? Perhaps the most dramatic events in the Arab Awakening await their climactic Last Act.[59]

1 Stephen M Walt, 'Why the Tunisian revolution won't spread', Foreignpolicy. com, 16 Jan 2011. **2** Cited by Paul Mason, *Why It's Kicking Off Everywhere*, Verso, 2012. **3** Yasmine Ryan, 'The tragic life of a street vendor', Al Jazeera English, 20 Jan 2011. **4** Tim Gee, *Counterpower*, New Internationalist, 2011. **5** Paul Mason, op cit. **6** Miniwatts Marketing Group, Internet World Statistics: Africa, 31 Dec 2011. **7** Quoted by Yasmine Ryan, 'How Tunisia's revolution began', Al Jazeera English website, 26 Jan 2011. **8** 'Tunisia security forces shoot dead protester', BBC News website, 25 Dec 2010. **9** 'Tunisian jobs protests reach capital Tunis', BBC News website, 28 Dec 2010. **10** 'Scores hurt in Algeria protests', Al Jazeera English website, 30 Dec 2010. **11** 'Deadly riots in Tunisia shut down schools', CBS News website, 13 Jan 2011. **12** Protests continue in Tunisia', Al Jazeera English website, 26 Dec 2010. **13** 'Tunisia unrest spreads to capital', Al Jazeera English website, 11 Jan 2011. **14** 'Tunisia: President Zine El Abidine forced out', BBC News website, 14 Jan 2011. **15** Noam Chomsky, speaking on *Democracy Now*, 17 Feb 2011.
16 'Egyptians protest over minimum wage', Al Jazeera English website, 3 May 2010. **17** George Lakey, *Toward a Living Revolution*, Peace News Press, 2012. **18** George Lakey, speaking at Friends House, London, 16 Jul 2012. **19** Hossam el-Hamalawy, 'Egypt's revolution has been ten years in the making, *The Guardian* website, 2 Mar 2011. **20** Ian Black, 'Egypt accused over crackdown on protests', *The Guardian*, 25 Mar 2003. **21** Wael Ghonim, *Revolution 2.0*, Fourth Estate, 2012. **22** James L Gelvin, *The Arab Uprisings*, Oxford University Press, 2012. **23** Mark Le Vine, 'Tunisia: How the US got it wrong', Al Jazeera English website, 16 Jan 2011. **24** Robert Fisk, 'The brutal truth about Tunisia', *The Independent,* 17 Jan 2011. **25** Asmaa Mahfouz, speaking on Memri TV, 2 Feb 2011. See youtube.com/watch?v=2uzdOLXLoes **26** Quoted by Tim Gee, op cit. **27** Quoted by Alex Nunns and Nadia Idle (eds), *Tweets from Tahrir*, OR Books, 2011. **28** 'Bahrain workers fired for supporting protests', Al Jazeera English website, 6 Apr 2011. **29** 'UK arms sales to Middle East include tear gas and crowd control ammunition to Bahrain and Libya', Campaign Against Arms Trade news release, 17 Feb 2011. **30** 'Saudi women given voting rights', Al Jazeera English website, 25 Sep 2011. **31** Peter Beaumont & Robert Booth, 'Bahrain used UK-supplied weapons in protest crackdown', *Guardian* website, 17 Feb 2011. **32** 'Saudi Arabia uses UK-made armoured vehicles in Bahrain crackdown on democracy protesters', Campaign Against Arms Trade news release, 16 Mar 2011. **33** Richard Norton-Taylor, 'London arms fair faces protest from anti-weapons trade campaigners', *Guardian* website, 12 Sep 2011. **34** David Blair, 'Arab Spring "anti-democratic" says Benjamin Netanyahu', *Daily Telegraph,* 24 Nov 2011. **35** Cited by Paul Mason, op cit. **36** 'Haaretz poll: Netanyahu losing public support over handling of Israeli housing protests', *Haaretz*, 26 Jul 2011.
37 Carlo Strenger, 'Israel's secular middle class strikes back', *Guardian* website, 2 Aug 2011. **38** Harriet Sherwood, 'Israeli protests: 430,000 take to streets to demand

social justice', *Guardian* website, 4 Sep 2011. **39** Dimi Reider, 'J14 may challenge something even deeper than the occupation', *972* magazine, 7 Aug 2011. **40** Ronny Edry, speaking on 'Israel's Radical Left', Vice TV nin.tl/SkXyz2 **41** 'Israeli protester sets himself on fire at rally', *Guardian* website, 14 Jul 2012. **42** George Brock, 'The power of social, networked media in Tunisia', undated blog (accessed 13 Sep 2012). See nin.tl/X0YzBy **43** Viktor Mayer-Schonberger, speaking on BBC TV Newsnight, 17 Jan 2011. **44** Evgeny Morozov, 'First thoughts on Tunisia and the role of the internet', ForeignPolicy.com, 14 Jan 2011. **45** Quoted by Firas Al-Altraqchi, 'Tunisia's revolution was Twitterized', *Huffington Post*, 14 Jan 2011. **46** Phil England, 'Fear no more: Power of the People' (interview with Gigi Ibrahim), *New Internationalist*, May 2011. **47** Yasmine Ryan, 'How Tunisia's revolution began', Al Jazeera English, 26 Jan 2011. **48** 'Palestinian inmates in Israel end mass hunger strike', BBC News website, 14 May 2012. **49** 'Voters register for Saudi municipal elections', Al Jazeera English website, 23 Apr 2011. **50** Rami Zurayk, *Food, Farming and Freedom: Sowing the Arab Spring*, Just World Books, 2012. **51** Betsy Leondar-Wright, *Class Matters*, New Society Publishers, 2005. **52** Tariq Ramadan, *The Arab Awakening*, Allen Lane, 2012. **53** Melanie Phillips, 'On Egypt the left are all neo-cons now', *The Australian*, 15 Feb 2011. **54** Dima Khatib, 'Love, not hatred, dear Mona!', blog, 24 April 2012 (accessed 15 September 2012). See nin.tl/Sl5mAO **55** John Naughton, 'Yet another Facebook revolution: Why are we so surprised?', *The Observer*, 23 Jan 2011. **56** Abdul Nabi Shaheen, 'Saudi women defy ban to register for polls', *Gulf News*, 26 Apr 2011. **57** Jason Burke, 'Saudi Arabia women test driving ban', *Guardian* website, 17 Jun 2011. **58** 'Saudi Facebook activist planning protest shot dead', *Middle East News*, 2 Mar 2011. **59** Anthony McRoy, 'The Arab Awakening', *Third Way*, Sep 2012.

5

Camping on the doorsteps of power

From Climate Camps to Tahrir Square, from Indignados to Occupy, the humble tent has become a vital accessory to modern resistance movements. But just as integral to these protests has been cutting-edge communications technology – and their success may lie in the creative tension between online and physical space.

When the London Olympics began in July 2012, signs at the front of the 'Olympic Park' listed items that were banned on site. One of them was 'demonstration articles or items'. It was accompanied by a picture of a tent.[1]

A year earlier, few people in Britain – or most of the world – would have thought to symbolize 'demonstration equipment' with a tent. But this was the time of the Occupy movement and the Indignados, when the world's financial élites found public anger camping on their doorsteps.

The internet played a central role in many of these protests: initiating them, keeping them going and even hosting passionate debate about the problems with them. At the same time, these movements returned to old-fashioned practices that seemed to have disappeared from modern politics – public meetings, equal decision-making and putting goals for the future into practice in the here-and-now. The link between these two apparently incongruous images holds the key to understanding these movements.

European summer

The biggest cause of the camping protests that got under way in 2011 was, of course, the economic crisis of 2008 and the austerity measures that followed it. Without other factors, such as the internet and the Arab Spring, the reality of unemployment, inflation and cuts would almost certainly have triggered mass protests. However, the other factors made a real difference to the form that these protests took.

Other campaigns had already done the groundwork. Occupy protesters made great use of the sort of 'hashtag activism' that was explored in Chapter 3. They drew on the experience of the Uncut movement, which was among the first to campaign against austerity. They were inspired by the Arab Spring, particularly the occupation of Cairo's Tahrir Square. The Arab Spring encouraged people around the world to believe that they too could topple political and social orders that had looked like they would last forever.

It would be a mistake, however, to see the outbreak of public occupations in 2011 as simply a romantic desire to emulate the activists of Egypt. Few people would spend many nights in the rain, risking their health and freedom, for the sake of an emotional whim. By 2011, the economic crisis was not only hitting people hard. It was also exposing the gap between the very rich and the rest. Conventional political mechanisms were failing to give most people a voice. The link between money and power was becoming ever more obvious. With the coming of the Indignados and Occupy, the link could no longer be ignored.

In the West, the protest camps of 2011 began not in New York – as is sometimes mistakenly reported – but in Spain. Spanish activists were discussing issues and tactics via the internet-based group *Democracia Real Ya* (Real Democracy Now), or DRY. As the Egyptian crowds gathered in Tahrir Square in February, members of DRY met in Madrid and planned a major demonstration. It would take place on 15 May, a week before regional elections.

On that unforgettable Sunday, thousands of Spaniards rallied in the Puerta del Sol, a square in central Madrid. Police put the number at 20,000; DRY said it was 50,000. There were simultaneous protests in over 50 other Spanish cities and towns. More than 500 organizations declared their support, although DRY were keen to avoid identification with any one party or group.

Spain's youth unemployment rate had reached 46 per cent. The ranks of the protest were swelled by large numbers of young people new to activism. But the protesters did not confine themselves to talking about jobs and cuts. They made the link to questions of political accountability. DRY chose the slogan 'We are not goods in the hands of politicians and bankers'. This is key: the Indignados and Occupy movements both refused to separate issues of money and power.

DRY had called the demonstration as a one-day protest. But the police responded brutally. A few demonstrators resorted to smashing windows. At the end of the day, a number of protesters refused to leave the Puerta del Sol. They held group discussions and organized into smaller groups to find food and sleeping equipment. Using smartphones, they set up the Twitter hashtag '#acampadasol'. They managed to stay in the square until the morning, when the police chased them out.

Naturally, some wanted to occupy the square again. In pre-internet days, they might have worried that there would be too few of them. But now numerous messages on Twitter and Facebook made clear that many were determined to sleep in the square the next night. This time, around 200 people turned up.[2]

Two days later, there were nearly a thousand people camped in the square. The police obtained a court ruling allowing them to remove the camp. On Saturday 21 May, less than a week after the protest began, there were 25,000 people occupying the Puerta del Sol.[3] Another 35,000 were protesting and camping in other squares across Spain.[4] Whereas the first actions had been called and co-ordinated by DRY, many were now appearing spontaneously. Like the Uncut movement before them, they often declared their membership of the movement with Twitter hashtags. Activists held regular assemblies in the squares to make decisions by consensus. Small solidarity demonstrations appeared in Lisbon, London, Athens and other European cities.

'La Puerta del Sol in Madrid is now the country's Tahrir Square,' wrote Spanish activist Pablo Ouziel. 'The "Arab Spring" has been joined by what is now bracing to become a long "European Summer".'[5]

Spanish anger, it seemed, was here to stay. Protesters called themselves the Indignados – the 'indignant ones' – or the 15-M movement, after the day that it all began. The hashtag '#Spanishrevolution' became common on Twitter. As protest continued, the 'indignant' Spaniards aimed their slogans directly at the rich and powerful: they chanted 'If we can't dream, you won't sleep'.

We are the 99%

The message and creativity of the Indignados reached a long way. On 30 July 2011, Malaysian activists gathered in Dataran Merdeka – a public square in Kuala Lumpur – and stayed overnight. Using the language of 'participatory democracy', they held a public assembly to debate political and economic issues. They cited both the Arab Spring and the Indignados as inspirations. In a distinctive tactic, they rejected continuous occupation and instead resolved to meet and stay in the square every Saturday night. The practice spread to other squares in Malaysia.[6]

On 2 August, the Indignados voluntarily left the Puerta del Sol. But if Spain's politicians and bankers breathed a sigh of relief, their satisfaction was short-lived. The Canadian magazine *Adbusters* called for an occupation of the financial district of New York: Wall Street. The call spread rapidly on the internet.

On 17 September, around 1,000 people walked up Wall Street to protest against the power and actions of the financial élite. Between 100 and 200 camped overnight in nearby Zuccotti Park. Within a week, at least 80 arrests had been reported.[7] And then, with the political right hoping that the media would not give the protests too much coverage, the YouTube revolution showed that it was alive and well. Footage emerged of a police officer, Anthony Bologna, pepper-spraying a protester who was already penned in and could not move.

The image provoked outrage, securing Occupy Wall Street both publicity and sympathy. Cyberactivists spread satirical images online that portrayed Bologna spraying his can in various famous historical settings. Clyde Haberman wrote in the *New York Times*, 'If the Occupy Wall Street protesters ever choose to recognize a person who gave their cause its biggest boost, they may want to pay tribute to Anthony Bologna'.[8]

Like the Indignados before them, the occupiers of Wall Street quickly made the link between money and power, between economic justice and real democracy. They insisted that the real divide in the US and in the world is between the very rich and the rest. 'We are the 99%' became the movement's dominant slogan. There are conflicting accounts of its origin. The idea was soon helped along by a report from the Congressional Budget Office showing that, despite the economic crisis, the richest one per cent in the US had doubled their share of national income over the past 30 years.[9]

Other occupations broke out across the US and 'Occupy America' was born. Once again, hashtag activism was used by groups forming spontaneously in their own towns and cities. They declared their existence on Twitter, followed by '#Occupy'. On 11 October, Occupy Mexico City began. Some months before, the Indignados had called for a global day of action on 15 October. On that day, around 200,000 marched in Madrid. In Rome – one of the few places in which there were violent as well as peaceful protests – activists launched Accampata Roma, their own equivalent of Occupy and the Indignados. In Frankfurt, hundreds of protesters began Occupy European Central Bank. Swiss campaigners rallied outside banks in Zurich. In Hong Kong, a protest camp began next to the international headquarters of the HSBC. Over 6,000 protesters gathered in Brussels. The call to Occupy London Stock Exchange led to clashes with police after protesters were prevented from camping on the privately owned land nearby. They chose the nearest available alternative: the area in front of St Paul's Cathedral.

The protests of 15 October were not confined to financial centers. That night marked the beginning of Occupy Auckland, Occupy Copenhagen and far too many others to list. A new network called Taking Back South Africa led to protest camps in Johannesburg, Cape Town and Durban. By 29 October, there were estimated to be Occupy camps in over 2,000 towns and cities worldwide.[10]

The global nature of the movement hit home after police violently evicted the Occupy Oakland camp in California on 25 October. People in Egypt, who had overthrown a dictator only eight months previously, demonstrated outside the US embassy in Cairo to declare their support for the occupiers. While activists in different countries have always shared messages and encouragement, the use of the internet made their communication both quicker and easier. Mexican activists sent a message to 'our brothers and sisters in struggle on the other side of the border'. They declared 'Together and in concert we are toppling this miserable system'.[11] Occupy Wall Street considered sending a delegation to Egypt. Activists in Cairo responded, 'Any time you do want to come over, we've got plenty of comfy couches available. It won't be fancy, but it will be fun.'[12]

The day after the Egyptians sent the message, Occupy Wall Street was forcibly cleared from Zuccotti Park by police. The camp in Zurich was evicted on the same night, 14 November.[13] Occupy London Stock Exchange held out through a series of legal battles before being cleared by police in the early hours of 28 February 2012. Members of the anti-capitalist group Christianity Uncut (myself included) were dragged by police from the steps of St Paul's Cathedral while kneeling in prayer.[14] Occupiers in Hong Kong managed to hold out until 10 September before being forcibly removed from outside the HSBC.[15]

Naming the elephant

By the middle of 2012, most Occupy camps had disappeared. Many on the political right had regarded Occupy as either naïve or dangerous. They now celebrated its demise.

Their celebrations were premature. Similar protests continued to appear. Occupy Nigeria began in January 2012, aimed at tackling corruption and unrepresentative government. On 15 May 2012, a year after the beginning of the Indignados movement, thousands marched in Spanish cities to renew their demands for change. The next week, the government of Quebec responded to student protests over tuition fee increases by bringing in a law restricting protest. In one of the biggest acts of civil disobedience in North American history, nearly half a million people defied the new law and marched through Montreal. There followed months of student strikes and the defeat of the Quebec government at the polls.[16] In June, the Radical Left Coalition, or Syriza, came close to winning the Greek general election. Other European governments denounced Syriza and effectively blackmailed the Greek people by saying they would not receive a bailout if they did not implement massive cuts. Despite this, Greece came closer to electing a radical leftwing government than any other country in the European Union's history.[17]

The Indignados and Occupy, like the Uncut movement, significantly shifted public debate in a number of countries. With Uncut, the shift had often been around tax avoidance and thus about alternatives to austerity. Now it was about the nature of power itself.

Occupiers were frequently accused of not having specific demands. A number of camps did produce lists of aims and post them online, some far more concrete than others. However, this criticism misses the point. Occupy was not about presenting the powerful with a list of requests. It was about challenging their right to hold power at all. The language of the '1%' and '99%' emphasized that the real division in society is between the very rich and the rest. This challenged attitudes which put the blame for poverty on the poor, or set public-sector workers against private-sector workers or the Global South against the Global North. It undermined attitudes to class divisions that contrasted the middle class with the working class, rather than seeing them both as exploited by the super-rich. A century and a half earlier, Karl Marx had predicted that those in the middle would gradually become indistinguishable from the working class and that their major conflict would be with the small number at the top of society. The Occupy movement generally did not use the language of Marxism. Indeed, some occupiers strongly objected to Marxist ideas, while others embraced them.

Nonetheless, a major contribution of Occupy was to frame politics in terms of a conflict between two classes. As George Lakey puts it:

> '2011 was the right historic moment for Occupy to present its meme about the 1%, but receptivity to a message is also conditioned by the deep habit of acquiescence; the public was used to the Elephant in the Room and the few people naming it were getting nowhere. The brilliance of Occupy was not only in the framing but also in the boldness of presentation: the choice to do nonviolent direct action while naming the elephant... Occupy turned on the light and provided another lesson in the art of revolution.'[18]

A major feature of the Occupy and Indignados movements was their ability to recruit new people to activism. Some of these came via networks such as Twitter and Facebook, when activists sent messages or videos to less politically engaged friends who became supportive. On the other hand, the influx of homeless people into many camps, some of whom were walking past and joined spontaneously, shows that not everyone needed the web to find Occupy.

The diversity of people involved in the Indignados and Occupy is an achievement in itself, for a campaign that only involves hardened campaigners is unlikely to succeed. Spanish broadcaster RTVE estimated that between 6.5 million and 8 million Spaniards have taken part in Indignados protests (the Spanish population is just over 47 million).[19] Paul Mason notes that the Occupy movement in Britain included a broader range of participants than UK Uncut. In particular, he thinks that there were more working-class people involved.[20] Chris Rossdale, who was part of Occupy London Stock Exchange, says he 'met people who had never been actively involved in campaigning, which was awesome and doesn't happen nearly often enough'. He adds that the camp 'had also gone some way to dealing with divisions between "old timers" and new faces, which isn't an easy task'.[21] Ian Chamberlain, who lived at Occupy London Stock Exchange for two months, says that the camp drew people who felt marginalized by mainstream politics and the traditional left. He adds that discovering people with shared problems and concerns, and building up trust while living in a community together, marked 'an end to alienation for a lot of people'.[22]

The international nature of the protests, and the increasing tools of global communication, added to their strength. Yannar Mohammad, of the Organization of Women's Freedom in Iraq, described Occupy and related movements as a 'second wave of global revolutions' after the Arab Spring. In a message from her group to Occupy Wall Street, she wrote: 'Creating such a movement globally was beyond even the wildest dreams of most visionaries, but has proven to be within reach in 2011. And your #Occupy movement has played a leading role in igniting it.'[23]

Tensions within the movement

While the internet played a central role in organizing and publicizing Occupy camps, it was also important for discussions of their problems. It would be naïve and untruthful to suggest that the Occupy movement had no negative aspects. Many of these centered around decision-making and inclusivity. At some camps, consensus decision-making worked well. At others, it began to break down. Similarly, it was clear that there were different views on the meaning of inclusivity. Sami, who was active in Occupy camps in London, told me that there was a 'lack of understanding of how the spaces perpetuated societal issues such as sexism, racism, homophobia, and their intersections'.[24]

Such criticisms were fairly common. At Occupy Boston in the US, a group of women occupiers read out a statement arguing that the camp had been operating without a feminist perspective and thereby ignoring its purpose. 'If you're not talking about sexism and racism, you're not talking about economic justice,' they insisted.[25] Naturally, the statement was posted online. As a result, it rapidly traveled around occupiers and other activists, both in the US and internationally, contributing to debates on gender, race and inclusion at Occupy camps. While such issues were discussed at camp assemblies, they also provoked heated debate on Twitter, Facebook and blogs – particularly on the part of people who felt that their perspective had been ignored in the assemblies.

A number of bloggers wrote about feeling excluded as queers, trans people or people of color. Disabled activists berated the lack of access at certain Occupy camps. Some argued that working-class people had been welcomed only in theory and not included as equals. Debates over gender and sex became particularly heated in Scotland, following allegations of sexual assault at Occupy Glasgow.

For some, these problems were a reason to give up on Occupy. Scottish feminist blogger Kate Harris went so far as to call for an end to the Occupy Edinburgh camp, citing antisemitic and sexist language and male dominance of decision-making.[26] Others felt things could change. Rinku Sen, a prominent feminist and anti-racist campaigner in the US, argued that the original Occupy organizers 'didn't consciously reach out to communities of color at the beginning; as a result, many people of color felt alienated'. Nonetheless, she added that 'local movements seem able to self-correct – and some newer occupations have been racially conscious from the start'.[27]

Rinku Sen argued that the issue was not simply about diversity but about the way in which occupiers saw the world and the issues that mattered to them. Occupy America faced criticism almost immediately from Native Americans on the grounds of its name. 'We are reminded that the territories of our indigenous nations have been "under occupation" for decades, if not centuries,' declared the American Indian Movement of Colorado. 'In the US, indigenous nations were the first targets of corporate/government oppression'.[28] Their statement was unanimously endorsed by Occupy Denver.

Other activists suggested that terms such as 'decolonize' or 'reclaim' were preferable to 'occupy', although in most cases the word 'occupy' remained. In the same way, feminists and queer activists in Spain and Latin America have objected to the term 'Indignados', which is a male noun in Spanish. Some use the word 'Indignadxs' by way of a gender-neutral alternative.[29]

Many occupiers have argued that a recognition of the movement's weaknesses cannot be separated from the wider struggle in which it is engaged. A group of Quakers who worshiped every week at Occupy London Stock Exchange noted that: 'Occupy has struggled to deal with many of the problems caused by the social and economic system which they seek to change: alcohol and drug abuse, male domination of meetings, homelessness, those suffering from mental illnesses and other broken people living in a broken world.' They added: 'We uphold their efforts to deal with these problems in good faith and with compassion.'[30]

The way in which these debates were carried out says a lot about the Occupy movement generally. On the one hand, the issues were debated at the camps themselves. On the other, there were global internet discussions. Some took to the internet because they felt their perspectives had been ignored at camp assemblies. Others accused them of doing so because the decisions at assemblies had gone against their own position.

The tension between online and physical space is central to any understanding of Occupy, the Indignados and related movements. It would be wrong to see them as entirely, or even primarily, internet-based phenomena. Hashtag activism played its part. As with the Uncut and Slutwalk movements, anyone could write '#Occupy' on Twitter when they wanted to start a camp. But there was a difference. Uncutters and Slutwalkers sought to gather people together in a specific location only for a brief period. In contrast, occupiers could start their camps and invite people to join them over time.

A sort of marriage

If we want to understand the role of the internet in Occupy and the Indignados, we need to look back much further than 2011. There is a lot to be learnt from earlier protest camps.

As Tim Gee puts it, 'On the face of it, camping does not seem like the most likely tactic to bring about the transformation of power relations in society. But it has frequently played a role in movements for change.'[31] Occupying physical space has long been a way of making a point. Often, the point it's making is that the space rightly belongs to those who have turned up and sought to stay there. In Latin America in particular, rural activists have frequently taken over land and declared that it is they, rather than the wealthy landlords, who really own it.

In other parts of the world, the tradition is an old one but less often mentioned. In 1649, members of the Digger movement occupied St George's Hill in Surrey in England. They built huts and began to farm the land. They developed a radical Christian theology that saw private property as sin. The Diggers were violently suppressed by an alliance of landowners, politicians and religious leaders. Troops were sent in tear up their corn and destroy their cottages.

In 1906, thousands of people camped outside the British Embassy in Persia to call for greater democracy. In 1932, working-class residents of Sheffield and Manchester in the north of England organized a 'mass trespass' of Kinder Scout, a vast area of rural beauty whose aristocratic owner denied them the right to walk, hike and camp there (six were imprisoned, but the law was changed on access to the countryside).[32] In the 1980s, British activists camped outside military bases, most famously at Greenham Common in Berkshire. In the 1990s they set up tents in the path of new motorways (and the government abandoned plans for 77 new roads). After the invasion of Iraq, George W. Bush was faced with an anti-war camp outside the White House. French campaigners against immigration controls established the No Borders camp at Calais.

Around this time, protest camping took off internationally in the form of the Camp for Climate Action, better known as Climate Camp. The first Climate Camp was held at an international summit in Scotland in 2005. Soon, there were Climate Camps at British power stations. Several involved direct action to interrupt the work going on there. The movement rapidly went global, with Climate Camps in Australia, New Zealand/Aotearoa, India, Ghana and Ukraine, as well as North America and most of northern and western Europe.[31]

Historically, many activist camps have been lived-out protests. On the one hand, they called for a new society based on different principles. On the other, they sought to run their camps by these same principles in the here-and-now. The Diggers believed that God had 'made the Earth to be a common treasury', so they resolved to treat it as such immediately by farming land together and sharing property.[33] The French activists at No Borders believed that migrants should be given better advice, so they provided an advice service at their own camp. The Climate Campers thought that decisions should be made by consensus, so they made their own decisions by consensus.

Direct action, in the original sense of the phrase, is about doing something that you believe to be right without waiting for those with power to give their permission. As we saw in Chapter 3, the Slutwalkers asserted their right to walk around freely, dressed as they wished, by doing just that. Many activists quote Gandhi's encouragement to 'be the change you want to see'. It is important to realize that this is not about withdrawing from the world to live out a utopian lifestyle. At its best, it is about living in a way that points to a much wider change and makes that change more likely.

Protest camping goes further than most direct action in that it involves communities – however small or short-lived – seeking to operate by the same principles that they are calling on society as a whole to adopt. As British occupier Sam Halvorsen put it, the places created by Occupy 'exist as much in our mind as our actions'.[34]

Non-hierarchical working has been a key aim of the Indignados and Occupy. In practice, as we have seen, some camps did better than others at operating in truly non-hierarchical and inclusive ways. It remained a key aim of the movements. In some areas, occupiers acted on their belief that education should be non-hierarchical by running public classes and seminars. Those occupiers who had been involved in Climate Camp and Uncut drew on their previous experience of large-scale consensus decision-making. Others expected non-hierarchical working because of their experience of hashtag activism and online discussion.

There is a tension between the two images of Occupy – online debates spinning round the globe and open meetings in public squares. It appears a bizarre mixture of old-fashioned habits and very new methods. To understand this paradox, we need to appreciate the importance of the rejection of hierarchy. Both these practices differ from electoral politics in most Western countries today. They both provide space for people to be heard whose concerns rarely appear in Congress or Parliament. In both cases, the relative equality is open to abuse. Both public assemblies and Twitter debates can be dominated by a few influential voices. But at their best, they enable levels of equality and inclusivity that have no place in mainstream political debate. Ian Chamberlain describes Occupy as 'the best example we've seen so far of a sort of marriage between the online world and the offline world'.

A year after the beginning of the Indignados movement, veteran anti-war activist Howard Clark described this approach:

> *'I now live in Madrid and last year, 2011, when I attended my first neighborhood assembly of the 15-M (the Spanish 15 May movement of "Indignados"), I felt a shiver of excitement to hear a plea for patience with consensus decision-making; "we're moving slowly because we want to go far". A year later, I cannot generalize about this diverse movement or assess what its long-term impact might be, but I know the difference it has already made in the neighborhood where I live – stopping home repossessions by the banks whose chiefs are not suffering from the crisis, occupying the disused offices that were once a Job Center, bringing a sense of excitement, creativity and even playfulness to almost every area of struggle and showing that themes of protest are connected... Nonviolent revolution is not the work of an instant. But from the continuing protests in Egypt and Bahrain, through the Indignados in Spain and the anglophone "Occupy movements"... the central task is to set about building here and now the world we want.'*[35]

1 'Westfield and Olympic site visit', protestlondon2012.com 13 July 2012.
2 Gianpaolo Baiocchi and Ernesto Ganuza, 'No Parties, No Banners: The Spanish experiment with direct democracy', Feb 2012, reproduced in *Dreaming in Public: Building the Occupy movement*, edited by Amy Schrager Lang and Daniel Lang/Levitsky, New Internationalist, 2012. **3** BBC News website, 'Spain: Protesters defy

ban with anti-government rallies', 21 May 2011. **4** Giles Tremlett, 'How corruption, cuts and despair drove Spain's protesters on to the streets', *Guardian* website, 21 May 2011. **5** Pablo Ouziel, 'Spain's Tahrir Square', *Political Affairs* website, 18 May 2011. **6** Alyaa Alhadjri, '"Occupy Dataran" ends peacefully', *The Sun Daily*, 16 Oct 2011. **7** Colin Moynihan, '80 arrested as financial district protest moves north', *New York Times*, 24 Sep 2011. **8** Clyde Haberman, 'A new generation of dissenters', *New York Times*, 10 Oct 2011. **9** Robert Pear, 'Top earners doubled share of nation's income, study finds', *New York Times*, 25 Oct 2011. **10** Chris Barton, 'Occupy Auckland protest speaks with many voices', *New Zealand Herald,* 29 Oct 2011. **11** 'Solidarity Statement: We walk by asking, we reclaim by occupying', 13 Nov 2011, reproduced in *Dreaming in Public*, op cit. **12** 'Response to OWS Egypt delegation proposal', 13 Nov 2011, reproduced in *Dreaming in Public*, op cit. **13** 'Arrests made at Occupy protests in US cities', Al Jazeera English website, 18 Nov 2011. **14** Jerome Taylor and Charlie Cooper, 'Unoccupied: Life after the camp', *The Independent*, 29 Feb 2012. **15** 'Occupy Hong Kong camp cleared from HSBC headquarters', *Guardian* website, 11 Sep 2012. **16** Richard Seymour, 'Quebec's students provide a lesson in protest politics', *Guardian* website, 7 Sep 2012. **17** Helena Smith, 'Greek elections: Antonis Samaras faces tough task to forge unity', *The Guardian*, 18 Jun 2012. **18** George Lakey, *Toward a Living Revolution*, Peace News Press, 2012. **19** 'Spain braces for anti-austerity rallies', *Hispanic Business*, 1 May 2012. **20** Paul Mason, speaking at the Netroots UK conference, London, 30 Jun 2012. **21** Chris Rossdale, interviewed 16 Aug 2012. **22** Ian Chamberlain, interviewed 1 Oct 2012. Other quotes from Ian Chamberlain in this chapter are from this interview. **23** Yannar Mohammad, Organization of Women's Freedom in Iraq, 'Message of solidarity to Occupy Wall Street', 3 Nov 2011, reproduced in *Dreaming in Public*, op cit. **24** Sami, interviewed 17 Aug 2012. **25** Occupy Boston Women's Caucus, 'Statement', 18 Nov 2011, reproduced in *Dreaming in Public*, op cit. **26** Kate Harris, 'De-Occupy Edinburgh', on her blog beyoungshutup.wordpress.com 11 Nov 2011. **27** Rinku Sen, 'Forget diversity, it's about "occupying" racial inequity', *The Nation,* 14 Nov 2011. **28** American Indian Movement of Colorado, 'An indigenous platform proposal for "Occupy Denver"', 9 Oct 2011, reproduced in *Dreaming in Public*, op cit. **29** Amy Schrager Lang and Daniel Lang/Levitsky, *Dreaming in Public*, op cit. I have cautiously decided to stick with the terms 'Occupy' and 'Indignados' to describe these movements, as these are the terms used by most of the people who have started them and in most discussions about them. However, I accept the criticisms of the terms and am open to being challenged. **30** 'Epistle from the Quaker Meeting for Worship at Occupy the London Stock Exchange', 4 Mar 2012. **31** Tim Gee, 'Past Tents: A brief history of protest camping', *Bright Green Scotland* website, 30 Oct 2011. **32** Dave Toft, 'Occupy Kinder Scout', *Red Pepper,* Aug 2012. **33** Gerard Winstanley, 'The True Levellers' Standard Advanced' in *Radical Christian Writings: A reader*, edited by Andrew Bradstock & Christopher Rowland, Blackwell, 2002. **34** Sam Halvorsen, 'Occupying Everywhere: A global movement?' in *Occupied Times*, 11 Feb 2012. **35** Howard Clark, *Making Nonviolent Revolution*, Peace News Press, 2012.

Cyberactivism explodes

From mass online petitions by the likes of Avaaz and 38 Degrees to YouTube protests like Pussy Riot, cyberactivism is breaking new ground. But even as it takes us into virgin territory, it throws up important new questions – not least about the value of 'clicktivism' and about the impact of the internet on minority languages.

An Israeli called Ronny Edry logged onto Facebook in March 2012 and set up a page called 'Israel loves Iran'. The Israeli Prime Minister Benjamin Netanyahu had just spoken of war with Iran. Iran's President, Mahmoud Ahmadinejad, had responded with equally aggressive rhetoric. Edry added posters to the page declaring 'Iranians: We love you' and 'We will never bomb your country'.[1]

Within days, another page was set up by people in Iran. It was called 'Iran loves Israel'. Iranians posted on Edry's page to say 'Israelis: We love you.'

In the coming days and weeks, thousands of people clicked that they 'liked' the pages – while others expressed their anger and disapproval. Other posters were soon designed and placed on the page. They included pictures of Israelis telling their government that they were 'Not ready to die in your war'. There were images of Israelis and Iranians side by side, declaring 'We love you'. In October 2012, the page's supporters ran a series of public posters in Tel Aviv. Each featured an Israeli and an Iranian declaring their love for each other's people.

'I never met an Iranian,' Edry explained. 'It's always the same here in the Middle East – we have so many enemies and we don't know any one of them. I just wanted to check with them, the day-to-day people, like me. Are they feeling the same? Are they afraid?'[2]

One of the first posts from Iran declared, 'For there to be a war between us, first we must be afraid of each other, we must hate. I'm not afraid of you, I don't hate you. I don't even know you.'[3]

In pre-internet days, it was not unknown for peace activists whose governments were in conflict with each other to work together. The Fellowship of Reconciliation, one of the oldest pacifist organizations in the world, was set up at the outbreak of World War One by small numbers of German and British Christians. They rejected the pro-war rhetoric of their churches' leadership and declared: 'We can never be at war'. Argentinean peace activist Adolfo Pérez Esquivel traveled to Europe in 1982 when his country was at war with the UK. He wanted to meet British anti-war groups, but the UK authorities denied him entry. British peace campaigners traveled to France to meet him.[4]

Such events are rare. War often relies on the ideas and values spread by the powerful, whose people have little if any personal contact with the people on the other side of the divide. The campaign that began with Israel-loves-Iran and Iran-loves-Israel raises the intriguing possibility that governments' plans for war could be undermined by their citizens meeting directly on the internet and standing up against leaders on both sides.

It is doubtful if this campaign could have happened without the internet. This can now be said for a number of other movements. There are others that may well have taken place without the net, but would have taken a very different form. It's worth asking what difference the internet has made to the effectiveness of campaigns that have relied on it. To help us consider the question, I have chosen two other examples, also from 2012.

Disabled cyberactivists defeat the UK government

The press galleries in the UK Parliament were quiet on the evening of 11 January 2012. The House of Lords was expected to rubber-stamp the government's proposals to cut social security for disabled people. Most newspapers did not bother to send a reporter to hear peers debating the issue. Nothing newsworthy was expected to take place.

In rapid succession, the Lords threw out three key elements of the government's proposals. They voted to reject frequent re-testing of disabled people, to retain entitlement to certain benefits for young disabled people unable to work, and to exempt cancer patients from benefit time limits.[5]

The BBC displayed the news on its website in the briefest terms while its journalists struggled to discover what had happened. Most newspapers were unprepared for the possibility of a government defeat and had made no provision for covering the story. The shock result appeared to have come out of nowhere.

'They had no idea we were going to win,' said leading disability activist Sue Marsh. 'Watching lobby journalists rushing around trying to find peers to ask what was going on was a sight to behold.'[6]

The few journalists who were less surprised were those who had been closely following Twitter and cyberactivism. In the days leading up to the vote, disability campaigners had mounted a massive online campaign targeted at specific members of the House of Lords. It was undoubtedly one of the most effective internet-based campaigns ever to take place in Britain.

The campaign had been building for a long time. Following the general election of 2010, the new coalition government had announced multi-billion-pound cuts to the welfare budget as a central part of their austerity drive. Benefits for disabled people were a particular target. Rightwing newspapers filled up their front pages with stories of 'scroungers' who falsely claimed to be disabled. Prime Minister David Cameron stated that people who applied for disability benefits previously had been given them with 'no questions asked'.[7] In fact, claimants already had to go through rigorous tests and a government investigation had revealed a fraud rate of only 1 in 200.[8]

Tests for disabled people claiming Employment Support Allowance were carried out by Atos, a transnational company accused of conducting simplistic assessments with the aim of cutting as many benefits as possible. Countless stories emerged of people forced to miss meals and turn off heating after their benefits were removed. The group Disabled People Against Cuts (DPAC) says that hundreds of people have died not long after being declared well enough to seek employment.[9]

As vast swaths of disabled people lost their income, government-supporting newspapers gleefully reported the figures as evidence that many claimants had been fraudsters all along.[10] They ignored the more detailed evidence. Over 40 per cent of appeals against Atos were upheld. The figure rose to 70 per cent in the case of claimants accompanied by a legal adviser.[11] Alongside cutting disability benefits, the government was also planning to cut access to legal aid, meaning fewer claimants would be able to seek legal advice.

Between them, the media prejudice and the Atos assessments rapidly contributed to a climate of fear. Disability charities reported a sharp increase in the number of disabled people experiencing verbal abuse in public.[12] Many disabled people felt that they had become a particular target of both government cuts and media hatred.

By late 2011, when a number of disabled activists and bloggers began to work together on a new report, they decided to promote it online. It seemed that even left-of-center newspapers did not regard disability benefits as a newsworthy issue. They submitted a series of requests under the Freedom of Information Act and devoted hours to analyzing the results. They asked to see responses to a government consultation on scrapping Disability Living Allowance. It turned out that many aspects of the government's proposals were opposed by over 90 per cent of respondents, with one measure opposed by 99 per cent. One document revealed that the Conservative Mayor of London, Boris Johnson, had criticized the proposals, a fact he had not made public.

The results were released in a report on 9 January 2012, entitled *Responsible Reform*.[13] In practice, it was known as the 'Spartacus Report'. Supporters of the ancient Roman rebel leader Spartacus are said to have all claimed to be him, to make it impossible for the authorities to arrest Spartacus alone. Disabled activists and their allies now used the slogan 'I am Spartacus' to emphasize that attacks on disabled people could affect anyone. It was published with the backing of disability charities and the Ekklesia thinktank, but it was social-media users who led the way. It took about half an hour for '#spartacusreport' to be 'trending' on Twitter.

By midnight at the end of 9 January, three million tweets had been sent about the Spartacus Report. The Ekklesia website crashed due to a record number of visitors.

In the following days, campaigners sent targeted tweets and emails to individual members of the House of Lords who they thought were persuadable. Many of them were 'cross-benchers', those peers who sit independently, siding permanently with neither the government nor the opposition. Most of the mainstream media remained unaware of this until the government defeat three days after the report was published.

Finally, television news programs started to take the issue seriously. Sue Marsh, one of the report's lead authors, was invited to appear on the BBC's flagship current affairs program *Newsnight*. Later, reflecting on the speed of the campaign, she said, 'Two years ago, remember, I hadn't even had a blog. I didn't know what a blog was. And now I was on *Newsnight*.'[6]

The next week, the government avoided a defeat on a fourth aspect of the bill by only 16 votes, after telling the Lords that a delay would cost £1.4 billion ($2.2 billion) – a figure for which they proved unable to provide evidence.[14] The following

Saturday, disabled people took to the streets, blocking Oxford Circus in central London by locking their wheelchairs together in an action supported by UK Uncut. Rosemary Willis of Disabled People Against Cuts (DPAC) insisted, 'We will not let this government push through these changes, which have already led to disabled people taking their own lives'.[15]

Ministers were determined to ignore both cross-bencher peers and wheelchair users chained across roads. They invoked the right of the House of Commons to override the Lords and used their majority in the Commons to push through their original proposals. The Welfare Reform Bill had not, after all, been blocked.

That certainly does not mean that the campaign had been worthless. Prior to the Spartacus Report, cuts to disability benefits were not regarded as a major political or media issue in Britain. Afterwards, everything changed. Disabled activists regularly appeared on TV and radio and their street protests hit the headlines. This is not to say that this happened as often as it should have done given the seriousness of the issue, but the difference was remarkable. When DPAC and UK Uncut called for a week of action against Atos in August 2012, their protests made front pages.[16] By the time that hundreds of activists blockaded Atos' London offices on 31 August, ministers had learnt to their cost that disabled people were not an easy target.[17]

Punk singers take on Putin

'Egyptian air is good for the lungs/ Do Tahrir on Red Square!' sang eight brightly dressed women as they danced opposite the Kremlin in January 2012, protesting against Vladimir Putin's presidential election campaign.[18] Wearing multi-colored tights and colorful balaclavas, they were members of the feminist punk band Pussy Riot. Formed in 2011, they had begun with anti-government songs performed on underground trains, backing greater democracy, freedom to protest, feminism and gay and bisexual people's rights. The Kremlin protest was their most public performance to date and YouTube clips of it rapidly spread around Russia and elsewhere.

Meanwhile, Patriarch Kirill I, primate of the Russian Orthodox Church, described the rule of Vladimir Putin as 'a miracle from God'. Others suspected a far more human intervention in the electoral process after Putin was returned to the presidency on 4 March. Thousands took to the streets in response to widespread allegations of vote-rigging. Kirill I denounced the protesters – some of whom were members of his own Church.

The protests had been building up during the election campaign itself, with many insisting that it would not lead to a fair result. On 21 February, shortly after Kirill I's 'miracle' comment, five members of Pussy Riot entered Moscow's Cathedral of Christ the Savior. They removed their winter coats to reveal their brightly colored clothes, including balaclavas to hide their identity. They approached the altar, crossed themselves and began to dance. At this stage, they did not sing, contrary to many inaccurate media reports. Within minutes, they were forcibly removed from the building.

Shortly afterwards, they released a clip of the incident on YouTube, dubbed over with a song framed as a prayer to St Mary the Virgin, a central figure of devotion in the Orthodox Church. 'O Virgin Mother of God, put Putin away!' they sang. The song attacked 'The Church's praise of rotten dictators/ The cross-bearer procession of black limousines'. It insisted that 'Mary, mother of God, is with us in protest'.[19]

It was the use of YouTube, combined with their creative and colorful style, that made Pussy Riot's performances globally known. Even then, they would be considerably less well known today were it not for the reaction of the Russian authorities and the Orthodox Church leadership. In the weeks following the protest, three women in their twenties – Maria Alyokhina, Nadezhda Tolokonnikova and Yekaterina Samutsevich – were arrested and charged. They all admitted that they were among the dancers in the cathedral, but passionately defended their right to protest peacefully against what they regarded as an illegitimate government.

Kirill I described the protest as 'blasphemous' and linked Pussy Riot with the Devil.[20] Vsevolod Chaplin, a prominent rightwing priest, accused Pussy Riot of 'Satanic rage'[21] and said he knew that God had condemned them.[22]

The three defendants were denied bail, although two of them were mothers of young children. Their cause received a boost when they were defined as 'prisoners of conscience' by Amnesty International.[23] Pussy Riot's online supporters ensured that news of the arrests was discussed on social media. The hashtags '#pussyriot' and '#freepussyriot' became common on Twitter. The band received backing from Western celebrity singers such as Madonna and Paul McCartney, some of whom were concerned particularly with artistic freedom.

The trial provoked heated debate about links between church and state. Nikolai Polozov, one of the lawyers acting for Pussy Riot, was a devout Orthodox Christian and criticized the Church's leadership for being too close to government.[24] Other Orthodox Christians strongly condemned Pussy Riot and called for harsh punishment, while some criticized the protest but urged forgiveness and leniency.

Mainstream media in the West had paid little attention when the women were arrested, but by the time they came to trial it was a major news story. It is hard to be sure why the level of interest changed so quickly. In part, it can be put down to the reality that a trial is more interesting than an arrest. Furthermore, at the time of the cathedral performance, it was only one anti-Putin protest among many. However, the growing global support for Pussy Riot was also a factor in pushing it up the media agenda. The celebrity endorsements were undoubtedly part of this, although Pussy Riot made clear that the millions of unknown supporters on Twitter were just as valuable. An anonymous member of the band said, 'We're flattered, of course, that Madonna and Bjork have offered to perform with us. But the only performances we'll participate in are illegal ones. We refuse to perform as part of the capitalist system.'[25]

The treatment of the singers was condemned by various governments, some of whom were longstanding critics of the Putin regime. Pro-Putin bloggers took to the internet to accuse Pussy Riot of being 'dupes of American hegemony' and said that the US had meted out far worse treatment to its own political prisoners.[26] But some of Pussy Riot's Western backers were just as critical of their own governments as they were of Putin. Keith Hebden, a Christian anarchist and Church of England priest, suggested that Pussy Riot could tour the UK because 'their message would certainly ring as true here as it does in Russia'. He criticized the leadership of his own Church as well as the Russian Orthodox Church and insisted that 'The established church will always crucify dissenters eventually'.[27]

As the trial went on, it became harder to dismiss the singers as naïve, uneducated, pro-Western or anti-Christian. Alyokhina quoted John's Gospel and analyzed the Orthodox Church's use of a passage about blasphemy.[28] Samutsevich told the court: 'In our performance we dared, without the Patriarch's blessing, to combine the visual image of Orthodox culture and protest culture, suggesting to smart people that Orthodox culture belongs not only to the Russian Orthodox Church, the Patriarch and Putin; that it might also take the side of civic rebellion and protest in Russia.'[29]

As the judge sentenced the three women to two years each in a penal colony, the treatment of Pussy Riot was almost universally condemned outside Russia. This small group of punk feminists had used creativity and YouTube to make known their message about the links between the Putin regime and the Russian Orthodox leadership. Thanks to the regime's over-reaction, this message was now hitting front pages around the world. As the singers were led away in handcuffs, it was clear that the people who had really lost this fight were Vladimir Putin and Patriarch Kirill I.

Solidarity

At first glance, these three examples seem very different. However, they all involved small groups of people making their concerns known to millions. They were all noticed by mainstream media only after becoming major phenomena online. In the case of the Spartacus Report and Pussy Riot, they appeared spontaneous but followed careful preparation and a thoughtful choice of tactics. They invited people who were not directly affected by a particular injustice to stand in solidarity with those who were.

Experience and planning were important. All three convicted members of Pussy Riot had activist experience long before their cathedral protest. Ronny Edry is a graphic designer, meaning he has the skills to design the posters that formed the main feature of the 'Israel loves Iran' Facebook page. The producers of the Spartacus Report established a 'Twitter rota' for the day of the report's release, dividing the day into two-hour periods and agreeing that each of them would tweet about it during their allocated time slot. They also identified specific members of the House of Lords whom it would be beneficial to target. Like other effective activists – such as UK Uncut and the Slutwalk movement – they drew on a mixture of experienced campaigners, people with detailed knowledge of the issues and newcomers with the passion that could energize others.

Like Pussy Riot, many other activists have used the internet to ensure that their protests are seen by far more people than were present when they took place. The Reclaim Shakespeare Company, based in Britain, is an activist group that campaigns against the transnational oil firm BP and its sponsorship of the Royal Shakespeare Company. On 23 April 2012 (the date usually given as Shakespeare's birthday), activists in Elizabethan costume climbed onto the stage a few minutes ahead of a performance of *The Tempest* in Stratford-on-Avon. They performed a two-minute sketch in Shakespearean language about BP's role in environmental destruction and called on theatres not to accept sponsorship from oil firms. They were applauded by a considerable proportion of the audience before leaving the stage so that the play could begin.[30]

They carried out similar acts of 'anarcho-thespianism' at other events sponsored by BP in the following months. When preparing their sketches, they made a priority of ensuring that they would be filmed. By posting the film clips on YouTube, and spreading them via other social media, the number of people who see the protest is multiplied several times over.[31]

The usefulness of the internet for publicizing these actions should not be underestimated, but nor should we ignore its limitations. Activist film clips are most likely to be passed around amongst activists. Some of those who see Pussy Riot on the underground, or the Reclaim Shakespeare Company briefly taking over a stage, will be hearing about certain issues for the first time. People who see them online are more likely to be already sympathetic. However, they can still play a role in turning armchair supporters into campaigners.

Further, campaigns that start on social media tend to become widely known only after they have achieved coverage in mainstream media. But the very fact that social media can lead to mainstream media coverage says a great deal about what online activists can do. This is all the more likely when they are as organized and effective as those who produced the Spartacus Report. They publicized it on Twitter, but focused on those decision-makers whom they were most likely to influence. In the early days of the British anti-cuts movement, many anti-cuts activists were unaware of the specific impact of the cuts on disabled people – but keen to support them once they heard the facts. Kerry Owen, a mental-health activist in the north of England, found she needed to explain the ins and outs of government changes to particular benefits in order to gather active support. 'It's very technical and you really have to go into detail,' she says. 'You need to be a policy geek.'[32] The Spartacus Report managed to cover complex issues in detail, while channeling a far broader message about the overall impact of the cuts on disabled people.

Effective use of the internet can help a marginalized group or small-scale campaign to attract empathy and support from people who are not directly affected. Whether in the form of non-disabled people declaring 'I am Spartacus' on Twitter, or Pussy Riot supporters wearing multicolored balaclavas outside Russian embassies in New Zealand/Aotearoa, they show those who wield power that they are taking on a far bigger group of people than they had imagined.

Communities whose needs and identity are not recognized in mainstream media or dominant values have used the internet to connect with others, to give voice to their own concerns and to challenge stereotypes. As with Israel and Iran, groups *within* countries have used the web to distance themselves from the dominant views in their own country. An Iranian writing on the 'Iran loves Israel' Facebook page declared to Israeli readers: 'Somebody every day threat[ens] me on the TV, to attack my country... I'm sure he does not represent all of Israelis. If you see someone on your TV talking about eliminating your country from the earth, you can be sure he does not represent all of us at all.'³

Similarly, the internet can be used to make clear that not all members of a religious, political or cultural community share the views of its leadership. Gary R Bunt, who has been monitoring Muslims' relationships with the web since its early days, says, 'The nature of the internet has encouraged marginalized Muslims, whose perspectives might not always be interpreted as "Islamic", to develop a voice and networking capability online'.³³ Examples include the 'Queer Jihad' site, operating since 2001 and promoting the equal acceptance of gay and bisexual people within Islam (the word 'jihad' means 'struggle', despite its frequent misuse by both Islamic fundamentalists and Western commentators who equate it with 'holy war'). Irshad Manji, a lesbian feminist Muslim, rose to prominence with her website Muslim Refusenik, before becoming known as an author of books calling for reform of

Islam. In Britain, the Christian web-based thinktank Ekklesia has challenged capitalism and war, promoted progressive approaches to sexuality and called for Christian institutions to give up their remaining privileges in UK law.[34] In doing so, it has undermined common assumptions about what Christians believe as well as providing space for debate among Christians who share some or all of its perspectives.

In 2003, Jenny Pickerill of the University of Leicester published one of the first major academic studies on cyberactivism in Britain, based on interviews with a range of environmental activists. She found that views on internet access amongst her interviewees varied wildly from those who saw the internet 'as accessible only to an élite few' to those who 'considered that access was universal'.[35] As we saw in Chapter 1, the numbers of people with internet access have grown considerably since then. Nonetheless, issues of access cannot be overlooked. Access levels vary within as well as between countries. In much of Europe, older people are less likely to be able to use the internet, even if they can afford to do so. This has implications for older people campaigning for their rights.

In some areas, much (or even most) internet use is now via mobile phones. Although richer countries tend to have higher numbers of mobile phones, the pattern is far more varied than in the case of internet use. For example, while internet access in Pakistan stood at nine per cent of the population in 2012, the country had over 119 million mobile phones (in a population of 180 million).[36] As more mobile phones are able to connect to the internet, optimists believe that this will mark the next big step forward in global access to the web.

There have been some imaginative attempts to campaign online in ways that don't exclude people without web access. Indymedia, which publishes activist news and resources online, has been known to send audio files over the internet that can be broadcast on local radio stations as well as to publish web-based text files that can be downloaded as flyers.[37]

Nonetheless, it is all too easy for activists who are in a relatively privileged position to forget that reliance on the web can exclude people who are often already marginalized. Addressing this reality may involve changing patterns of communication in order to be more inclusive. The British group Boycott Workfare took to making more decisions by phone calls and text messages because many benefit claimants could not afford easy access to the web.[38] This has not stopped them having considerable success with both online and offline campaigning (the next chapter looks at the group in more detail).

Language of resistance

We can't discuss the internet's role in excluding or including people without thinking about language. Pickerill found that newcomers could feel excluded by 'activists' slang'. She explained: 'Within a protest setting this may quickly become meaningful to the outsider, but if encountered through CMC [computer-mediated communication] alone it can serve as a form of exclusion'.[35]

In the same year as Pickerill's study, 2003, Pakistan's Minister of Information and Technology, Awais Ahmad Khan Leghari, bemoaned the English-language dominance of the internet. He insisted that 'with more that 95 per cent of Pakistan's literacy base in Urdu, the internet is relevant to only the country's élite five per cent'.[39] As Urdu content increased in the following years, some pointed out that even Urdu is not the first language of many Pakistanis, who often communicate primarily in more local languages.[40]

Speakers of localized and minority languages have given the web a mixed reception. In its early days, many feared that it would only hasten the increasing domination of influential languages such as English. They had good reason to think so: the onset of computing had already led to battles over language, with many languages opting for variations of English words when it came to terms such as 'computer'. The Danish language adopted the word *computari*. In the Faroe Islands, which are governed by Denmark, language activist Johan Poulsen created the alternative noun *telda* from a Faroese verb that means 'to compute'. The word caught on, but a later attempt to replace *kompaktdisk* with a Faroese-derived word, *ljomfloga*, was less successful.[41]

Some saw new technology as an opportunity to promote minority languages, because 'books, newspapers, discs and websites can be produced in small languages at minimal cost'.[42] Welsh speakers began developing materials that could be used online as early as 1993, ensuring that online dictionaries were in place by the time that use of the internet became widespread. Delyth Prys, involved in the early stages of the project, later argued that 'Such tools are a great help to writers in minority languages, who often don't have much confidence in writing in their native tongue because it is excluded from so much of official and public life'.[43]

The internet continues to pose a challenge to small and even medium-sized language groups. In 2010, over half of all internet communication was in either English or Chinese.[44] In 2012 it was estimated that of the time that Welsh speakers spent online, only one per cent was spent using Welsh language sites.[45] The rest is most likely to be in English. But the number of Welsh-language blogs is on the rise, reaching 400 in the middle of 2012 (the number of fluent Welsh speakers in the world is around 600,000). For some, minority-language blogging is itself a form of activism. Welsh blogger Ifan Jones says that he feels a responsibility to 'promote the use of the language on the internet'. He adds, 'Like Welsh language communities, the members of the Welsh blogosphere feed off each other's activity. The more there are, the stronger the community, the more web users will use the Welsh language.'[46]

The advent of social networking has given hope to those who want to use technology to defend endangered languages. Malawian software developer Edmond Kachale, who produces resources in the Chichewa language spoken in parts of southern

Africa, says that the use of Chichewa on Twitter and Facebook has encouraged young people to keep speaking the language.[47] Basque speakers collect Basque-language tweets together on one site,[48] and the technology for doing so has now been used to produce similar sites in Catalan and Welsh.[49] Kevin Scannell, professor of computer science at St Louis University in the US, monitors the use of minority languages online through his website, Indigenous Tweets. As the name implies, it records the number of tweets sent in indigenous languages, ranging from Kreyol Ayisyen, spoken in Haiti (over two million tweets sent by September 2012) to Gamilaraay, spoken in southeast Australia (one tweet sent by September 2012).[50]

Wikipedia has proved particularly popular with minority language speakers, as they can easily add articles in their own language. Indeed, the language with the highest ratio between the number of Wikipedia articles and the number of speakers is thought to be Aragonese. Only about 10,000 people in northeastern Spain speak it as their first language but, by the end of 2011, there were over 25,000 Wikipedia articles written in it (in contrast, English had about four million articles and roughly 400 million first-language speakers).[51]

When languages or linguistic rights are under threat, the very use of a language can challenge dominant values and assumptions. To use Tim Gee's phrase (as we saw in Chapter 1), it is a type of idea counterpower. In 2011, speakers of Chakma – used by about 600,000 people in Bangladesh and eastern India – launched a series of projects to make Chakma script available on the internet. They described the initiative as a case of 'online activism'.[52] Sometimes, the activist nature of minority language use is more explicit. Speakers of a number of indigenous languages in Africa have recorded short films in their language, not only to preserve their native tongues but to make others aware of their cause. These are viewed on mobile phones in communities in which few people can afford computers.[53] The actor Barbara Nolan has created a series of short online videos in Nishnaabe, an indigenous language spoken in parts of Canada. She aims to introduce Nishnaabe to new speakers while raising awareness of the language's decline. By portraying stories through visual as well as spoken means, Barbara Nolan believes that viewers will 'be able to understand the general meaning of the stories being acted out – without needing translation'.[54]

The Occupy movement (as we saw in the last chapter) became more inclusive than mainstream politics through its use of physical meetings as well as online debates. It would be naïve to imagine that the internet can solve all problems of inclusion. It would be equally silly to pretend that it does not offer solutions to some of them. Just as the internet can exclude people through language, so it can connect people who want to speak in their own language. Just as it can reinforce the dominance of languages used by the powerful, so it can be a tool of resistance for those asserting their linguistic freedom.

Beyond clicktivism

Some have asked if the Spartacus campaign is evidence that campaigns in the future will be fought and won entirely online. The answer is almost certainly 'no'.

Spartacus was rare and innovative in moving straight from the internet to a victory in a parliamentary vote. But it was rooted in a longstanding disability rights movement, helped by a strong community of disabled bloggers. While disabled people in Britain have been campaigning on the streets for years, some took to the internet long ago precisely because physical activism is less accessible to them. The movement that led to the Spartacus Report had been building up for years before that momentous evening in the House of Lords. The longer-term impact – in terms of public awareness of growing criticism of government policy – depended on the mainstream media coverage and wider campaigning that followed.

People who want to fight all campaigns entirely online make the same mistake as those who sneer at cyberactivism and think it can make no difference. They ignore the context. Issues are different, people are different, cultures are different and therefore campaigns must be different. Online petitions and the like sometimes attract sneering comments about 'clicktivism' and 'slacktivism'. Such criticisms are justified if it is claimed that these methods are the only ones needed. Evgeny Morozov is probably right when he says that most people who set up a Facebook page to promote a cause never go further than setting up the page.[55] However, the Spartacus Report, Israel-Loves-Iran and Pussy Riot are some of the many examples of campaigns that use the internet but go far beyond clicktivism.

Networks such as Avaaz and 38 Degrees, which organize web-based campaigning activities, have provoked widely varying reactions. I have come across people who regard them as the future of activism as well as others who see them as largely irrelevant and accuse them of promoting the idea that campaigning is easy. In reality, their methods can be successful if used as part of wider struggles.

In the weeks leading up to the London Olympics and Paralympics in 2012, it was pointed out that the Olympic Park was about to become one of the world's leading tax havens. Olympic sponsors would be required to pay no tax on their sales for the duration of the Games. 38 Degrees asked their supporters to email the companies directly, urging them voluntarily to pay the tax they would normally be charged. Before the Games were under way, four companies, including McDonald's and Coca-Cola, had agreed to pay their tax.[56] The online organizing of 38 Degrees doubtless contributed to their success, but it is unlikely that it would have had the impact it did had the issue of corporate tax-dodging not been made so prominent by UK Uncut. The companies may well have feared direct action had they not agreed.

As online petitions become ever more common, it is likely that the number of signatures that they will need to attract before making an impact will become higher and higher. This is perhaps a reason to make petitions more local or aimed at specific communities. Kerry Owen discovered a little known provision of York City Council that required it to debate any issue which gathered 1,000 signatures in a petition. By gathering enough signatures about cuts to disability services in 2011, she and her fellow campaigners ensured not only that the issue was debated but that it achieved local media coverage. 'It did mean we got a whole day with the lead item on BBC Radio York being about mental health,' she explains.

This sort of targeting is becoming increasingly important as activists – and friends of activists – risk being saturated with requests to sign petitions, retweet links and join Facebook groups. Several of the individuals most associated with cyberactivism are keen to stress that they do not see online campaigning as sufficient in itself. Egyptian activist Wael Ghonim ran the 'We are all Khaled Said' page on Facebook that was used as a rallying and organizing site during the Egyptian uprising of 2011. He has described the uprising as an 'internet revolution'. But closer attention to Ghonim's remarks reveals that he was clear about the site's purpose:

> 'The strategy for the Facebook page ultimately was to mobilize public support for the cause... The first phase was to convince people to join the page and read its posts. The second was to convince them to start interacting with its content by "liking" and "commenting" on it. The third was to get them to... contribute to its content themselves. The fourth and final phase would occur when people decided to take the action onto the street. This was my ultimate aspiration.'[57]

Processes such as these are described by Tim Hardy, who runs the 'Beyond Clicktivism' website, as a 'ladder of engagement', through which people move 'from Facebook "likes" to actual concrete action'.[58]

This is not to say that social media itself cannot be an important space for resisting injustice. Internet access is sharply increasing but, as we we are about to see, governments and corporations are becoming more and more aware of how to use the web to undermine people calling for change. This is the next big challenge for cyberactivism.

1 'Israel loves Iran', facebook.com/israellovesiran. 2 Ronny Edry, speaking on 'Israel's Radical Left', Vice TV. 3 'Iran loves Israel', facebook.com/IranlovesIsrael. OfficialPage/info 4 Symon Hill, 'Visit of Nobel Laureate', *The Friend*, 4 May 2012. 5 'Disability campaigners rejoice', *Ekklesia*, 11 Jan 2012. 6 Sue Marsh, speaking at the Netroots UK conference, London, 30 Jun 2012. 7 'David Cameron, Conservative Party conference speech', BBC News website, 5 Oct 2011. 8 'Disabled people point to issue of "benefit scroungers" as discrimination increases', Scope website, 31 Jul 2012. 9 'The closing Atos ceremony', Disabled People Against Cuts website, 30 Aug 2012. 10 'Sick benefits: 75% are faking', *Daily Express*, 27 Jul 2011. 11 Nina Lakhani, 'Paralympic sponsor engulfed by disability tests row', *The Independent*, 29 Aug 2012. 12 Peter Walker, 'Benefit cuts are fuelling abuse of disabled people, say charities', *Guardian* website, 5 Feb 2012. 13 See ekklesia. co.uk/responsiblereformDLA 14 'Government narrowly avoids a fourth Lords welfare reform defeat', *Ekklesia*, 17 Jan 2012. 15 'Protesters show anger over Welfare Reform Bill', BBC News website, 28 Jan 2012. 16 Nina Lakhani, 'Paralympic sponsor engulfed by disability tests row', *The Independent*, 29 Aug 2012. 17 Esther Addley and Shiv Malik, 'Atos protesters clash with police in "day of action" against Paralympics sponsor', *Guardian* website, 31 Aug 2012. 18 Miriam Elder, 'Feminist punk band Pussy Riot take revolt to the Kremlin', *Guardian* website, 2 Feb 2012. 19 There are varying English translations of the lyrics; these come from freepussyriot.org/video 20 'Pussy Riot reply to Patriarch', *Russia Today* website, 27 Mar 2012. 21 Simon Shuster, 'The priest who beat Pussy Riot', *Time*, Aug 2012. 22 '"God condemns Pussy Riot", Church official says', Orthodox Church Media Network, 26 Jun 2012. 23 Amnesty International press release, 4 Apr 2012. 24 Tom Esslemont, 'Russian Orthodox Church defiant over Pussy Riot trial', BBC News website, 11 Aug 2012. 25 'Remaining members of Pussy Riot: We're stronger than the state', Radio Free Europe website, 28 Aug 2012. 26 Paul Craig Roberts, 'Media Review: "Pussy Riot: The unfortunate dupes of American hegemony"', Orthodox Church Media Network, 27 Aug 2012. 27 Keith Hebden, 'Pussy Riot and the Kingdom of God', *A Pinch of Salt* blog (apos-archive.blogspot.co.uk) 17 Aug 2012. 28 'Masha Alyokhina's closing statement', Free Pussy Riot website, freepussyriot.org 29 'Katja Samutsevich's closing statement', Free Pussy Riot website. 30 Reclaim Shakespeare Company website, 'Protesters take to the stage at RSC over BP sponsorship', 23 Apr 2012. 31 Films of the performances can be viewed at nin.tl/TFgY49 32 Kerry Owen, interviewed 30 Aug 2012. Other quotes from Kerry Owen in this chapter are from this interview. 33 Gary R Bunt, 'Towards an Islamic information revolution?' in *Muslims and the News Media*, edited by Elizabeth Poole and John E Richardson, IB Tauris, 2006. 34 See ekklesia.co.uk 35 Jenny Pickerill, *Cyberprotest: Environmental activism online*, Manchester Univ Press, 2003. 36 'Mobilink leads market as mobile penetration touches', *Express Tribune*, 14 Mar 2012. 37 TV Reed, *The Art of Protest*, University of Minnesota Press, 2005. 38 Anne-Marie O'Reilly of Boycott Workfare, interviewed 14 Sep 2012.

39 Cited in Gary R Bunt, op cit. **40** Ivan Sigal, 'Pakistan: Internet and the challenge of language', globalvoicesonline.org 4 May 2010. **41** Mark Abley, *Spoken Here*, William Heinemann, 2003. **42** Daniel Nettle & Suzanne Romaine, *Vanishing Voices*, Oxford University Press, 2000. **43** Delyth Prys, 'The Welsh language's digital toolbox', globalvoicesonline.org 3 Aug 2012. **44** Miniwatts Marketing Group, internetworldstats.com/stats7.htm **45** Carl Morris, 'Imagining the Welsh language web', globalvoicesonline.org 31 Jul 2012. **46** Ifan Jones, 'The state of Welsh language blogging', globalvoicesonline.org 21 Jul 2012. **47** Kevin Scannell, 'Tweeting in Chichewa in southern Africa', rising.globalvoicesonline.org 27 Jul 2011. **48** See http://eu.umap.eu **49** See http://cy.umap.eu **50** indigenoustweets. com **51** Kevin Scannell, 'Language revitalisation through free software: The case of Aragonese', indigenoustweets.blogspot.co.uk 6 Dec 2011. **52** Rezwan, 'Online activism to save Chakma language', rising.globalvoicesonline.org 29 Nov 2011 **53** Rezwan, 'Promoting indigenous African language films', Global Voices, rising. globalvoicesonline.org 22 Nov 2011. **54** barbaranolan.com **55** Evgeny Morozov, *The Net Delusion*, Allen Lane, 2011. **56** Richard Murphy, 'That Olympic tax wheeze', 38 Degrees website, 30 July 2012. **57** Wael Ghonim, *Revolution 2.0*, Fourth Estate, 2012. **58** beyondclicktivism.com

7

Fighting corporations in cyberspace

The new communications technology may be used by protesters – but all the tricks of the trade are of course also available to transnational corporations and governments. 'Astroturfers' are infesting online debates, emails are being harvested and websites are being shut down. Battle in the ether has well and truly been joined.

In a London office at the end of 2006, the Campaign Against Arms Trade (CAAT) received an extraordinary email. It was from lawyers working for BAE Systems – one of the world's largest arms companies. BAE's lawyers said that they had seen an internal CAAT document concerning a legal challenge over BAE's arms sales to Saudi Arabia. Knowing that they legally had no right to this confidential document, they were now returning it to CAAT.

Reading the other side's confidential documents during a legal case is not a trivial matter. How had they gained access to it? How long had they been in possession of it? Did they have any other confidential CAAT documents? As CAAT investigated and took BAE to court, it was revealed that an agent hired by BAE had been spying on CAAT activists, probably by hacking into their emails.

It was not the first time that this sort of thing had happened. Four years previously, CAAT had discovered that a member of

their staff had been spying for BAE.[1] This time, after CAAT
began legal proceedings, BAE admitted that they had paid
£30,000 ($48,000) per year to a private investigator called
Paul Mercer to gather information on anti-arms activists. They
claimed that they had not expected him to do anything illegal,
although this claim was treated with derision in parts of the
media.[2]

This story is more personal to me than some of the other
incidents described in this book. I was one of CAAT's seven
paid staff at the time of the incident and my emails are likely to
have been hacked. Activists are used to the idea that the police
and other government agencies may be reading their emails, but
recent years have seen a stream of stories about corporations
using similar tactics. Here lies perhaps the biggest problem with
activist reliance on the internet: just as social movements can
use technology, so can corporations, governments and police.
And they can usually afford more expensive and more secretive
technology than is available to activists.

Big Brother is watching your inbox

Technology enables a lot of messages that would once have
been private to become publicly available – at least to those
with the money and skills to access them. That includes
governments that want to monitor opposition or suppress
human rights. In Cameroon, where laws discriminate harshly
against gay and bisexual people, a man called Roger Jean-
Claude Mbédé was imprisoned in 2011 for sending another
man a mobile phone text message reading 'I am very much in
love w/u [with you]'.[3]

Governments have been trying to censor the world wide web
for almost as long as it has existed. Censorship is considerably
more rigid in some countries than in others. The limits on
internet access imposed by the Chinese government have been
nicknamed 'the great firewall of China'. As early as 2005, *The
Guardian* estimated that about 30,000 people in China were

working for the internet police force.[4] According to Amnesty International, China has imprisoned more 'cyber-dissidents' than any other country in the world.

This has not stopped Chinese people using the internet to resist the state. In July 2012, the authorities abandoned plans to build a waste water pipeline in Qidong after thousands of people in the city protested over environmental damage. The protest was largely physical, but followed discussion of the proposal on Weibo, a Chinese microblogging site comparable to Twitter.[5]

Western governments are not immune to the desire to censor the internet. As we saw in Chapter 2, the head of London's Metropolitan Police considered switching off Twitter during the riots of 2011, before discovering he had no authority to do so. In 2012, the UK government introduced a Communications Data Bill to require internet service providers to keep records of all people's internet use, so that they could be accessed by police.[6] The same year, the US Congress threw out the Stop Online Piracy Act and the European Union rejected the Anti-Counterfeiting Trade Agreement. Both had been promoted as attempts to curb piracy online and to protect copyright, but were widely seen as paving the way for censorship.[7]

As time has gone on, governments have found that restrictions on the internet are harder to impose than they may have expected. Wael Ghonim, while running an anti-Mubarak Facebook page before and during the Egyptian revolution of 2011, used his technical skills repeatedly to change his online identity. The government were unable to work out who was really running the site.[8] Not every citizen who wants to challenge power is lucky enough to have this level of technical knowledge. Further, governments find censorship a lot easier when they have corporations helping them. There has been repeated criticism of leading technology companies for co-operating with the Chinese government's web censorship. Nick Cohen describes the Chinese firewall as a 'public-private partnership'.[9] During the Egyptian revolution, Vodafone sent pro-Mubarak text messages to its customers. The company said its staff had been forced to send the texts, although this is arguably the likely consequence of doing business with oppressive regimes.[10]

As well as helping governments to monitor resistance, many corporations are not above spying on activists in their own right. In January 2011, an investigation by the *Guardian* found a string of companies that were set up to provide information on campaigners. At least one of them was linked with Mark Kennedy, a former police officer in Britain whose identity was discovered only after he had spent years spying on environmental groups for the police. He later set up a shadowy company called Tokra, that appeared to have links to Global Open, a 'private security' firm. Global Open admitted to keeping a 'discreet watch' on protest groups for E-ON, a transnational energy firm. Its founder, Rod Leeming, said he had previously spied on animal rights groups as a member of the UK police's Special Branch.[11]

Legal concerns no doubt prevented *The Guardian* from naming too many of the companies that were involved in spying on campaigners, but it is clear that the case of BAE and CAAT is far from being a one-off. Methods of spying are varied. As with Kennedy's police work, there are cases of agents physically infiltrating activist groups. However, it would be naïve not to recognize that hacking is also likely to be a common practice.

Sometimes, sophisticated hacking skills are not necessary. If a campaigning group posts an event on Facebook, the police, government and corporations can read it as easily as anyone else. During the Arab Spring, a Saudi activist called Faisal Ahmed Abdul-Ahadwas was killed, allegedly by police, ahead of a planned day of protest he had publicized on Facebook.[12] Some campaigners have turned the situation to their advantage. At the beginning of the 2011 Egyptian uprising, activists posted false starting-points on Facebook for the protests in Tahrir Square.[13]

Campaigners frequently have to choose between the greater numbers and publicity that come with advertising an event in advance and the surprise value of concealing it until the last moment. A tactic that has become popular recently involves advertising one action while using it as a springboard for another action that has not been made public. In 2011, campaigners against the London arms fair discovered that the National Gallery in Trafalgar Square would host an evening reception for the arms dealers. This was supposed to be confidential information and the activists did not want anyone to know what they had found out. They used social media to publicize a protest at the offices of BAE Systems – a few minutes' walk from the Gallery. Once assembled there, they subtly spread the word among those who had joined the protest. Within a short space of time, there were a large number of protesters occupying the National Gallery, disrupting plans for the reception and ensuring that the arms dealers were greeted with a demonstration when they arrived.

Activist paradox

A paradox of cyberactivism is that it usually involves reliance on major corporations. Not only Google (which owns YouTube) but also Facebook and Twitter are major companies in their own right.

Ironically, corporations can end up facilitating discussion about campaigns aimed against them. Major web-based businesses such as Google and Amazon have been targets of the Uncut movement due to tax avoidance.

As commercial enterprises, companies Facebook and Twitter are likely to welcome business from most sources, including anti-corporate activists. There is much debate over whether such openness is reliable. During the Iranian uprisings of 2009, Twitter delayed a planned upgrade that would have temporarily shut down its site. They said that they did not want to hinder the Iranian activists using social media to resist the regime. It remains unclear whether or not the US government had asked the company to do this. If the US authorities can persuade Twitter to aid social-media activists in Iran, could they not also pressurize them to block activists in countries whose regimes have US support?

Such fears have grown as Twitter has given in to state pressure. In 2012, Twitter closed the account of the British anti-capitalist group, the Space Hijackers. The closure followed a complaint from organizers of the London Olympics, against which the group was protesting.[14] Twitter later agreed, after limited resistance, to give US police access to three months' worth of tweets sent by Malcolm Harris, an Occupy activist facing a criminal trial.[15]

The question is made harder to answer by the fact that social-media companies will naturally explain their decisions differently to their critics. In April 2011, the UK was preparing for a royal wedding. Fearing that leftwing groups would use the event as an occasion for protests, a number of activists were pre-emptively arrested and locked up for the duration of the wedding. Anarchist squats in London and Brighton were raided by police. Protesters on the day faced further restrictions and more were arrested.[16] At the same time, around 30 leftwing Facebook pages in Britain were closed down. Several UK Uncut groups, student activist networks and local branches of the Green Party found that their Facebook pages disappeared overnight. Facebook blamed technical problems, but offered no explanation as to why only leftwing groups appeared to have been affected, and at the same time as a police crackdown on radical campaigners.[17] No similar mass closure of radical pages seems to have taken place in Britain since this event, but that has not stopped campaigners fearing that it might.

Fears have been fueled by attempts by corporations to close down sites hosting critical discussions of their activities. This has been a favored tactic of Atos, a UK company that tests disabled people's eligibility for benefits. They have been widely accused by disabled activists of seeking to satisfy a government agenda of throwing people off benefits by inaccurately declaring them fit for work. In 2011, Atos threatened legal action against a website called After Atos. Their lawyers made the highly questionable claim that another site, called Atos Register of Shame, had a potentially libelous title.[18] A site called CarerWatch was shut down with no warning after Atos contacted its server host and alleged that a post on a discussion forum was libelous.[19] The site's purpose was to allow people who care for relatives to give mutual support to each other; it was not even an activist site.

There have been several attempts to get around the need to rely on corporately owned websites. Sites such as Z Communications and Global Voices have been set up to allow participants to share activist information. However, campaigners usually aim to involve new people who have not previously been politically active. Facebook and Twitter are helpful for this, even if activists send links that point them to other sites.

Impersonation and astroturfing

The corporate threat to internet freedom and cyberactivism goes beyond hacking and site closures. Recent years have seen corporations and even government agencies using the internet to give the impression that public opinion is in favor of policies that benefit the company or government concerned. These fake versions of grassroots activism have been dubbed 'astroturf' campaigns.

Early versions of this approach involved bombarding writers or discussion forums with comments that appear to be from large numbers of people objecting to their views. In reality, they may be sent by a much smaller number of people. Chinese authorities have for some time been paying people to post pro-government comments online.[20] As early as 2002, an investigation by Jonathan Matthews and Andy Rowell exposed the work of the Bivings Group, a US-based PR firm specializing in internet lobbying. An article on the company's website declared 'there are some campaigns where it would be undesirable or even disastrous to let the audience know that your organization is directly involved… it is possible to make postings to these outlets that present your position as an uninvolved third party'.[21]

Over time, such schemes have become more elaborate. Some now involve individuals establishing complex multiple identities online, with email, Twitter and Facebook accounts that all match up. Specialist technology has even been developed to make this easier. In 2011, it was revealed that the US Air Force had tendered for companies to provide it with software that would create 'ten personas per user, replete with background, history, supporting details and cyber presences that… can interact through conventional online services and social-media platforms'.[22] The next year, the US group Climate Progress revealed that John Droz, a leading climate-change denier, was involved in a plan to generate opposition to wind power. In a memo to his colleagues, he wrote that 'public opinion must begin to change in what should appear as a "groundswell" among grassroots'.[23]

The British campaigning journalist George Monbiot has been writing about astroturfing since 2002. He believes that the greatest threat to internet freedom and the 'global commons' of the web derives from these 'daily attempts to control and influence content in the interests of the state and corporations: attempts in which money talks'.[24]

Monbiot is probably right. As we have seen, attempts to censor the web have often been hard to enforce, but using the web for a fake version of what it is good at – spontaneous discussion from the ground up – stands a greater chance of being effective. As astroturfing tactics have become well known, activists and other web users have become more aware of how to spot them. Some suggest astroturf campaigns on Twitter seem to involve a lot of 'retweets' of original comments, whereas genuine grassroots feeling is more likely to make itself known in a higher number of original tweets. Unfortunately, as astrofurfing becomes ever more elaborate, the more sophisticated astroturfing campaigns are likely to take note of this.

Being aware of the dangers of astroturfing does not mean pretending that all genuinely grassroots activism is for progressive campaigns. It would be dishonest to pretend that supporters of the status quo cannot also engage in grassroots campaigning. In late 2011, the UK government announced that it would introduce legal recognition for same-sex marriage in England and Wales. The next year, the Scottish government declared that it would do the same in Scotland. The decisions followed longstanding grassroots campaigns for marriage equality, whose supporters welcomed the news.

Activism over the issue during the following months rarely involved physical protests but included a great deal of online campaigning. This included grassroots activism on both sides. The so-called Coalition for Marriage – made up predominantly of socially conservative religious groups – launched an online petition against same-sex marriage. In response, the Coalition for Equal Marriage – backed by human rights campaigners and progressive religious groups – launched a petition in favor of it. Other equality activists developed a site called Out4Marriage that filmed celebrities, politicians and religious leaders declaring their personal support for marriage equality. At the other end of the spectrum, hardline Protestants who objected to the multifaith nature of the Coalition for Marriage launched the Keep Marriage Special campaign, oddly encouraging their supporters to sign both their own online petition and the one promoted by the Coalition for Marriage.

Some equality activists found it difficult to believe that the campaign against same-sex marriage was a genuinely grassroots campaign, as they are used to fighting governments, corporations or right-wing groups with little presence on the ground. However, the anti-equality message was spread through conservative and middle-of-the-road churches (although more progressive churches spread the equality petition). Unusually for politics in Britain, this was a controversy in which both sides were able to mobilize genuinely grassroots activists.

Whereas astroturfing is about corporations impersonating activists, a fascinating inversion of the tactic involves activists impersonating corporations. Campaign groups have been known to set up websites that at first glance appear to be the sites of the companies they are campaigning against but which quickly turn out to be attempts to expose them. The idea is that people searching online for information on the companies will discover a less flattering view of them. Twitter accounts have been used in similar ways.

While these sort of tactics have been in use for years, they hit the headlines in summer 2012 over a site created by Greenpeace called 'Arctic Ready'. It was presented as being a site run by Shell to promote their plans for drilling for oil in the Arctic. The satirical nature of it became clear fairly quickly, with lines such as 'our money is worth more than any animals that used to live here'.[25] The site aimed to show what Shell was *implying* by its Arctic drilling plans, rather than what its directors were saying in public. What made the situation more unusual was Greenpeace's decision to run a fake Twitter account, @ShellisPrepared, that appeared to be Shell's social media team seeking to handle the bad publicity that arose from the site. There was also a video of what was supposed to be a Shell corporate social event gone wrong, but was in fact staged by Greenpeace. A number of people who posted the video on Facebook took it at face value. Further, with the Twitter feed implying that the site and video were real, there was considerable confusion and some web users were left unsure about what was true and what was not.

Science journalist Martin Robbins, writing in the center-left *New Statesman*, attacked Greenpeace for its methods. 'This is an NGO that thinks it is acceptable to lie to the public, to lie to bloggers and journalists,' he wrote. 'To behave in this deceitful way demonstrates an astonishing amount of contempt for the public – not least for environmentalist supporters who spread their message in good faith only to find themselves forced into embarrassing retractions'.[26]

Greenpeace seemed to be surprised that so many people had believed the site to be genuine. Greenpeace's Travis Nichols described it as 'an obviously satirical campaign'. He said that Greenpeace had not lied but had chosen to 'take the facts and put them out without Shell's spin. They've greenwashed their page. We've done the opposite. We took the language they used and flipped it.'[27]

While views on both the ethics and effectiveness of Greenpeace's action vary, it is clear that the freedom of the internet does not always allow those with the largest budgets to have the upper hand. The anonymity of the internet has advantages for people on both sides of a conflict.

Unemployed people defeating corporations

There are times when the wealth of corporations is no match for the anger of the people. The web does not make this happen, but it can speed up the process. In 2012, the British supermarket chain Tesco advertised a job – with no wage whatsoever. It was part of a government scheme requiring large numbers of unemployed people to work in exchange for their welfare benefits. Such practices had been common in the US for some time, where the term 'workfare' is often used. They were fairly new to the UK. Although the new government had significantly expanded these schemes in the previous two years, there had been little media coverage. Anne-Marie O'Reilly of Boycott Workfare says that it was difficult to interest people who were not personally affected.

'Their eyes tended to glaze over when we told them there was forced labor in the UK, like they didn't really believe us. There was hardly a single newspaper article about it.'[28] Over time, the group's campaigns and some minimal media coverage gradually increased awareness. But the issue really took off when social-media users expressed their outrage over the Tesco advertisement, posting it on Facebook and Twitter. The physical image of a job with no pay triggered both fascination and anger. The Boycott Workfare site received a record number of hits. Within a day, the mainstream media had picked up the story.

At that point, it turned out that the earlier groundwork was extremely helpful. O'Reilly explains: 'Because we were the only people who were already talking about it, our language became what was used. So the hashtag became '#workfare' whereas the government didn't want it to be called that. We got to frame the debate.' The group's website was not sophisticated. But it did list all the companies and organizations discovered to be using unpaid labor through the workfare schemes. They had used the Freedom of Information Act and ensured the list was accurate. Before long, all the companies concerned were receiving critical emails. Their Facebook pages were filled with comments challenging their participation in workfare.

These were not co-ordinated by Boycott Workfare, but were a case of spontaneous, autonomous campaigning on the part of unemployed people and others outraged by forced unpaid work. Whereas companies could delete critical comments on Facebook, the same cannot be done on Twitter. No-one is able to delete publicly visible tweets addressed to them. 'Twitter really changed the way that kind of thing happened,' says O'Reilly. 'On Twitter, there's much, much more pressure to respond quickly and to address the criticism.' As the online pressure built up, activists also occupied and picketed the stores of companies using workfare labor. Within a few weeks, a number of large companies – including HMV, TK Maxx and 99p Stores – had announced their withdrawal from the workfare schemes. O'Reilly believes that some of the companies would have responded this way based on the online pressure alone.

For others, the occupations and physical protests made the difference. Those that pulled out before this stage may well have feared the direct action that could be coming their way. The spirit – and fear – of UK Uncut was in the air.

A number of companies and charities are still taking part in the UK government's workfare schemes. The speed with which others have withdrawn has been remarkable, surprising campaigners as much as businesspeople and journalists. Boycott Workfare has skilfully combined the idea counterpower of the internet with physical and economic counterpower on the streets.

Like UK Uncut, the anti-workfare campaigners have needed little central organization once the anger of large numbers of people has changed the narrative. Their use of Twitter has been particularly clever and consistent, exposing companies to the public gaze and adding to the pressure with the fear of direct action. For all the corporate interference and government spies, for all the astroturfing and closure of websites, campaigns like this are a reminder that the web is, at its best, a place where the powerful really can be defeated by the passion and unity of the supposedly powerless.

1 Mark Thomas, 'Martin and me', *The Guardian*, 4 Dec 2007. 2 Rob Evans and David Leigh, 'BAE spy named by campaigners is friend of leading Tory', *The Guardian*, 19 Apr 2007. 3 All Out, 'One day to free Roger' , allout.org/en/actions/ roger 4 Jonathan Watts, 'China's secret internet police target critics with web of propaganda', *The Guardian*, 14 Jun 2005. 5 'China waste water pipeline scrapped after protest', BBC News website, 28 Jul 2012. 6 Brian Wheeler, 'Communications Data Bill creates "a virtual giant database"', BBC News website, 19 Jul 2012. 7 'Acta: Controversial anti-piracy agreement rejected by EU', BBC News website, 4 Jul 2012. 8 Wael Ghonim, *Revolution 2.0*, Fourth Estate, 2012. 9 Nick Cohen, *You Can't Read this Book*, Fourth Estate, 2012. 10 'Vodafone says Egyptian authorities forced it to send pro-Mubarak texts', *The Guardian*, 3 Feb 2011. 11 Rob Evans, Amelia Hill, Paul Lewis & Patrick Kingsley, 'Mark Kennedy: Secret policeman's sideline as corporate spy', *The Guardian*, 13 Jan 2011. 12 'Saudi Facebook activist planning protest shot dead', *Middle East News*, 2 Mar 2011. 13 Tim Gee, *Counterpower*, New Internationalist, 2011. 14 Emma Barnett, 'Twitter suspends Olympics protesters' account', *Daily Telegraph* website, 23 May 2012. 15 Matt Williams, 'Twitter complies with prosecutors to surrender Occupy activists' tweets', *Guardian* website, 14 Sep 2012. 16 Symon Hill, 'Arresting times', *The Friend*, 5 May 2011. 17 Shiv Malik, 'Activists claim purge of Facebook pages', *Guardian* website, 29 Apr 2011. 18 Stephen Sumpter, 'Atos moves to shut down criticism', latentexistence.me.uk 22 Aug 2011. 19 Jon Ronson, Lucy Greenwell & Remy Lamont, 'Carers versus Atos' attempt to protect its image', *Guardian* website, 6 Apr 2012. 20 Michael Bristow, 'China's internet "spin doctors"', BBC News website, 16 Dec 2008. 21 Quoted by George Monbiot, 'The fake persuaders', *The Guardian*, 14 May 2002. 22 George

Monbiot, 'The need to protect the internet from "astroturfing" grows ever more urgent', *Guardian* website, 23 Feb 2011. **23** Stephen Lacey, 'Memo: Group wants to create fake grassroots wind "subversion" campaign that "should appear as a groundswell"', Climate Progress website thinkprogress.org, 9 May 2012. **24** George Monbiot, 'These astroturf libertarians are the real threat to internet democracy', *Guardian* website, 13 Dec 2010. **25** See arcticready.com **26** Martin Robbins, 'Epic Shell PR failure? No, the real villains here are Greenpeace', *New Statesman* website, 18 Jul 2012. **27** Travis Nichols, interviewed by Kashmir Hill, *Forbes*, 19 Jul 2012. **28** Anne-Marie O'Reilly, interviewed 14 Sep 2012.

8

These hands are our weapons

Cyberactivism is not a magical cure-all – it is a tool like any other that can be put to good use or bad. But it is impossible to ignore – and much about our collective future will depend on how we harness the power of the internet to inspire resistance.

A woman whose name was never given stood in front of a tank during the Egyptian revolution, facing it head on. At that point it was unclear whether Mubarak would order the troops to fire on demonstrators and whether they would obey orders if he did. The woman told the British journalist Robert Fisk: 'If they fire on the Egyptian people, Mubarak is finished. And if they don't fire on the Egyptian people, Mubarak is finished.'[1]

It was an inspiringly brave comment for someone standing immediately in front of a tank. If the dictator could not use his troops to maintain control, he would lose power. But if he sent tanks against peaceful demonstrators, the resulting anger, civil disobedience and international pressure would ensure that his regime would not survive. Such courageous examples of 'nonviolence of the strong' give the lie to the notion that activism has become lazy in the age of the internet. Facebook and Twitter may have played their part in getting people to turn out in Tahrir Square and Wall Street, but once they were there, they needed as much dedication and solidarity as has always been required from activists for social and political change.

Simplistic explanations about the internet have abounded in recent years – from those who ignore economics and see technology as the cause of social change, to those who insist the net is irrelevant and fail to recognize its impact in informing, inspiring and mobilizing people. We must go beyond these one-sided perspectives that overlook the messy complexity of human behavior.

The former Chinese prime minister Zhou Enlai was asked in the 1970s if he thought that the French revolution of 1789 had been a success. He famously replied that it was too early to say. In 200 years, historians will still be debating the wave of activism that followed the economic crash of 2008. The relationship between activism, economics and technology may still be a live issue. People will know the answers to some of the questions that we are now asking. In some ways, they will be better placed to discuss them, but in other ways less so. History is a moving target. Those of us who are living through this wave of activism, and who have been part of it, need to reflect on it. If we do not, we are unlikely to be effective. What can we say about the role of the internet in the movements that this book has considered? And what can we say about the future?

Moving, not forming

The internet has not been the cause of this wave of activism. The economic crisis, accompanied by a range of individual historical and cultural factors, has a much greater claim to that title. But it would be wrong to suggest that the internet has not affected it. In some cases, it has equipped and emboldened people who might otherwise have remained silent. They range from Tunisians who could not see protests on state television but knew about them from Facebook, to Brazilian women who watched videos of Slutwalks online and decided to take similar action themselves. The internet has also made it easier to organize many forms of protest, speeding up communication and allowing activists to announce online the location of protests at short notice. The net has not replaced mainstream media nor is it less dominated by corporations than other forms of media and technology. This has not stopped activists turning it to their advantage.

The internet has also affected the form that activism has taken – sometimes in subtle ways that are difficult to assess. The net contributes to diversity, with rigid ideological groupings finding it as hard as corporations and governments to keep control of online narratives. The online dialogues between Iranians and Israelis who are committed to peace may turn out to be particularly important in the development of resistance to war.

Recent global activism has not been led by hierarchical organizations or sectarian groupings. Indeed, they have played very little part in it. Instead, movements have been formed from the ground upwards, often spontaneously. Opponents have smeared the Tahrir Square crowds as Islamist militants, the Uncut movement as middle-class layabouts, supporters of Slutwalk as exhibitionists and disabled activists as the stooges of extremists. One of the more bizarre claims made about Occupy London Stock Exchange was that it had been infiltrated by 'drunks, drug takers and Quakers'.[2] As I hope this book has demonstrated, none of these descriptions are true. Most of these movements have been initiated by people directly affected by the injustice in question, whether unemployment, corruption, dictatorship, sexual violence, homophobia or war. They have all benefited from the solidarity of those less directly affected than themselves. Undoubtedly, some of the movements described here have been more diverse and democratic than others. None of them have been without faults, some of them major.

It is not easy to say how much this lack of hierarchy is dependent on the internet. Spontaneous, non-hierarchical, grassroots movements have existed for centuries. During the 16th-century European Reformation, groups of radical peasants sprang up spontaneously across central Europe, working out political and religious ideas for themselves but making links with each other. Historians still debate the role of technology in this process: the invention of the printing press, and rise of relatively cheap printing, helped them to spread and share their views. It is also worth remembering that the internet can be used by hierarchical, corporate and governmental organizations as well as those who resist them. The web is not a magic antidote to hierarchy. Nonetheless, it has helped movements to spread in non-hierarchical ways. Once the Uncut, Slutwalk and Occupy movements were under way, publicized by both online and mainstream media, groups around the world declared themselves part of a global struggle by using the relevant hashtag and organizing a protest along roughly the same lines as others. The internet has made it easier for social movements to spread without the planning of a central international leadership.

The vast majority – but not all – recent activist movements have been nonviolent. Nonviolence is related to the non-hierarchical nature of recent activist movements. An army, by definition, is hierarchical. A movement that people can join in different ways, at different times, discussing issues on Facebook or in public squares, is unlikely to lead to the rigid hierarchy necessary for sustained violence. Active nonviolence is a natural choice for people seeking to build social and economic systems in which people relate to each other as equals, with mutual respect and a sharing of resources. It is also tactically sensible. As Gene Sharp puts it, activists who put their trust in violence have 'chosen the very type of struggle with which the oppressors nearly always have superiority'.[3]

Optimists suggest that grassroots movements will defeat institutions because institutions are too cautious and cannot respond as quickly as movements that are spontaneous, fluid and diverse. Institutions also tend to retreat into defensive mode, more concerned with preserving reputations or profits than with dialogue or even with gaining support. This is as true of institutional leftwing parties, trades unions and certain NGOs as it is of corporations and rightwing parties. It's no surprise that hierarchical socialist and communist parties were thrown off balance by Occupy and the Indignados, while anti-cuts campaigners have become frustrated with the slowness of mainstream trades unions. However, it seems unrealistic to suggest that movements will always defeat institutions. History presents a more mixed picture. The hierarchical nature of many institutions means that they can sometimes respond quickly because someone at the top makes a decision. Further, movements often fizzle out or turn into institutions themselves. As evidence of this, we have only to look at the number of religious groups that began as exciting alternatives to the mainstream only to turn into cautious, respectable institutions.

The internet has fueled an explosion of non-hierarchical movements in recent years. These movements now face a huge challenge. Will they gradually fade away? Will they turn into institutions, restrained by caution and a narrow focus? Will they continue as energetic, forward-thinking movements and, if so, how will they keep up their momentum? Will the internet help them to adapt, to take on new issues and tactics, without leaving other concerns behind? Will it help them to keep up the pressure where it makes the most difference? This may involve being ready to give up a particular name, label or organization for the sake of wider progress. It will mean being more concerned with moving forward than with forming fixed groupings or positions. It won't be easy.

On the net and on the streets

The future of politics and activism will be affected by developments in internet access and control. The majority of the world's population have never used the internet. It seems that the growth of mobile phone technology could fuel an international explosion in levels of access to the net, but this is not certain. The prospects for non-hierarchical social movements to spread via the internet will be affected for a long time by levels and types of access. Alongside this, crucial battles continue for the control of cyberspace. The format of sites such as Twitter and YouTube can make it hard for corporations to defend themselves from ridicule and awkward questions. But the growth of astroturfing shows that the powerful can also use the internet for their own complex strategies – and that many of them are becoming more familiar with effective ways of doing so.

These struggles will continue online because the internet is not separate from the fabric of life, politics and society. It is part of it. The same corporations that exercise influence over government and attack social movements in the media naturally behave in the same way on the web. Similarly, those who challenge their power on the streets can also confront them online. We cannot understand the role of the internet in politics and activism if we follow the lead of those who insist on seeing the net as existing on a different plane to other forms of communication. Like the printing press, radio and television, the net affects communication and activism, but it remains a platform for the same struggles of power and freedom that are going on outside it.

This is why effective campaigns can almost never be confined to the internet. Mainstream media coverage has played a number of vital roles in the recent wave of activism. This has ranged from Al Jazeera's coverage of protests in the Arab Spring to the international attention focused on Pussy Riot. Of course, there are exceptions. Online organizing allowed the Spartacus Report to alter a vote in Parliament before the mainstream media even noticed the issue. Once the vote had taken place, it became a big media story and this considerably increased its influence. I don't deny that most of the mainstream media generally upholds the status quo. Rather, I want to emphasize that engaging with and challenging mainstream media is usually at least as important as campaigning online – although the boundaries between the two are likely to blur over the coming years.

Resistance on the net needs to be accompanied by resistance elsewhere. Several recent movements have sought to live out the same ideas that they promote online. Public camps have tried to exemplify community, equality and shared decision-making. As participants in Slutwalks walked freely in the clothes they wanted to wear, they were doing the very thing that they were calling for the right to do. The idea counterpower of the net has been reinforced by physical and economic counterpower on the streets. It seems highly unlikely that corporations involved in the London Olympics would have so readily given up their tax exemptions if they had not been afraid of occupations and disruption in the style of UK Uncut. A major reason for the progress of the Uncut movement has been its ability to use nonviolent direct action to disrupt trade and profit. The revolutions in Tunisia and Egypt took a major step forward when protests were accompanied by strikes. I am not suggesting that strikes and direct action should be used indiscriminately. This is about choosing the most effective tactics in any given context. All too often, long-running campaigns, particularly in the UK and North America, are hampered by the lack of an economic element to resistance. With many trades unions led by cautious individuals committed to hierarchical structures, it is not yet clear to what extent they can act together with movements such as Uncut and Occupy. The use – or neglect – of economic counterpower is likely to have a bigger effect on the prospects for social change than the way that activists use the internet.

Mubarak and Ben Ali both offered limited concessions to protesters once it was far too late. Some have speculated that if they had made the offers much earlier, they would still be in power. By the time they tried to compromise, opposition forces had been given courage by seeing how far they had traveled. They could see victory in sight, and chose to push on until the regimes were overthrown. As austerity drives more and more people into poverty, the day-to-day struggle to exist may for many take priority over political action. On the other hand, it may spur them on to greater resistance. If concessions are won from pro-austerity governments, it remains to be seen whether people will push for greater change or settle for what they have got.

It is possible that activists' use of the internet could be one of the factors affecting their choice. Much has been made of the way in which the net 'shrinks' the world. It is easier than ever before to find out what is happening on the other side of the planet. Social movements that seek to keep up their momentum in difficult times should be able to use the net to learn from each other much more now than in the past. In the US in the 1970s, a group called the Movement for a New Society sought to build 'nonviolent revolution'. They provided training and facilitated skill-sharing as well as engaging in campaigns directly. They declared: 'Most of what we need to know to make a revolution, we have yet to learn'. One of the group's founders, George Lakey, revisited this slogan in 2012 and amended it to read: 'Most of what we need to know to make a revolution *is already within our global collective experience*. A lot of us haven't caught up with each other's learning. And new knowledge is waiting to be found.'[4]

Change lurking everywhere

At their early marches in Madrid, the Indignados waved their hands in the air and shouted 'These are our weapons!'[5] Their hands were used to make decisions by consensus in democratic meetings, to spread ideas and plan action online, and to liaise with each other across divisions of geography, class, religion and ideology. They were the weapons of a nonviolent grassroots movement. The possibilities that the internet provides for activism and social change are part of a much wider potential that has always existed. This is the potential realized by people who act together, refusing any longer to go along with the status quo, exercising counterpower that can be greater than the power of the small minority who control the tanks and the money.

In the words of Emmanuel Iduma, a founding member of Occupy Nigeria, 'There is change lurking everywhere'.[6] Of course, resistance to change is never far behind. Corporations and governments have as much interest in the future of the internet as do activists. As access expands, corporations will seek ever greater control, limiting online diversity, spying on campaigners, minimizing criticism and maximizing profits. There are many places in which the power of the 1% can be challenged by the 99% – on the streets, in Parliament or Congress, in the economy. Cyberspace is one of those 'places'. It is as dangerous to dismiss the importance of the internet as it is to regard cyberactivism as the cure for all our problems. We need to struggle on several fronts at once, with different tactics and prospects in different contexts. The internet is one battlezone among many.

In late September 2012, as I was finishing my work on this book, the Portugese government reversed a key austerity measure in response to mass resistance.[7] In the same week, a fresh wave of anti-cuts protests broke out across Europe. The people of Greece staged a one-day general strike. Public squares were again occupied in Spain. Thousands of people marched against austerity in Paris. Three months earlier, France had thrown out the rightwing President Nicolas Sarkozy. Many of those who marched were prepared to back his center-left successor François Hollande when they agreed with him, but this would not stop them speaking out when they thought he had become too close to the interests of big business. As trade unionist Annick Coupé put it, 'Just because we helped defeat Nicolas Sarkozy doesn't mean we're now going to shut up'.[8]

Since 2008, millions of people have experienced a taste of the freedom that comes with speaking out. From Tahrir Square to Wall Street, from the Slutwalks to the occupations of tax-dodging stores, from Facebook dialogue that crosses boundaries to YouTube clips that expose reality, from the fall of Ben Ali to the Quebec government's defeat over student fees, something extraordinary has happened. As inequality spirals, poverty deepens and corporations fuel climate chaos, there is a frightening amount to be done. We need more people speaking out, more clearly, more effectively and with more unity. This is not the time to shut up.

1 Robert Fisk, 'How much longer can Mubarak cling on?', *The Independent*, 31 Jan 2011. **2** Quoted by James Orr, 'Protesters want a break from cold and wet vigil', *Daily Telegraph*, 5 Nov 2011. **3** Gene Sharp, *From Dictatorship to Democracy*, Serpent's Tail, 2012. **4** George Lakey, *Toward a Living Revolution*, Peace News Press, 2012. **5** Gianpaolo Baiocchi and Ernesto Ganuza, 'No Parties, No Banners: The Spanish experiment with direct democracy', Feb 2012, reproduced in *Dreaming in Public: Building the Occupy movement*, edited by Amy Schrager Lang and Daniel Lang/Levitsky, New Internationalist, 2012. **6** Emmanuel Iduma, 'Is this the end of the Nigerian revolution?', 17 Jan 2012, reproduced in *Dreaming in Public*, op cit. **7** 'Portugal backs down on social security tax plans', BBC News website, 24 Sep 2012. **8** Kim Willsher, 'French protesters march in "resistance" to austerity,' *Guardian* website, 30 Sep 2012.

Bibliography

Firas Al-Atraqchi, 'Tunisia's revolution was Twitterized',
  Huffington Post, 12 Jan 2011, nin.tl/QqzU7H

Maria Alyokhina, Katja Samutsevich and Nadia
  Tolokonnikova, 'Closing statements', *Free Pussy Riot* website,
  13 Aug 2012, freepussyriot.org/documents

Andrew Chadwick, *Internet Politics: States, citizens and new
  communications technologies*, Oxford University Press, 2006.

Erica Chenoweth and Maria Stephan, *Why Civil Resistance
  Works: The strategic logic of nonviolent conflict*, Columbia
  University Press, 2011.

James Curran, Natalie Fenton and Des Freedman,
  Misunderstanding the Internet, Routledge, 2012.

Phil England, 'Fear no more: Power of the people' (interview
  with Gigi Ibrahim), *New Internationalist*, May 2011,
  nin.tl/VUThTd

Tim Gee, *Counterpower: Making change happen*, New
  Internationalist, 2011.

Wael Ghonim, *Revolution 2.0: The power of the people is greater
  than the people in power*, Fourth Estate, 2012.

Hossam el-Hamalawy, 'Egypt's revolution has been 10 years in the making', *Guardian* website, 2 Mar 2011, nin.tl/QqAFO7

Johann Hari, 'How to build a progressive tea party', *The Nation*, 21 Feb 2011, nin.tl/UnCk8q

Tim Hardy, Beyond Clicktivism' (blog), beyondclicktivism.com

Jonathan Heawood, 'There's more to protesting than "retweet",' *The Independent*, 20 Aug 2012.

Gigi Ibrahim, 'Tahrir and Beyond' (blog), theangryegyptian. wordpress.com

Farhad Khosrokhavar, *The New Arab Revolutions that Shook the World*, Paradigm, 2012.

George Lakey, *Toward a Living Revolution: A five-stage framework for creating radical social change*, Peace News Press, 2012.

Amy Schrager Lang and Daniel Lang/Levitsky (editors), *Dreaming in Public: Building the Occupy movement*, New Internationalist, 2012.

Leah A Lievrouw, *Alternative and Activist New Media*, Polity Press, 2011.

Alessio Lunghi and Seth Wheeler (editors), *Occupy Everything!: Reflections on why it's kicking off everywhere*, Autonomedia, 2012.

Toby Manhire (editor), *The Arab Spring: Rebellion, revolution and a new world order*, Guardian Books, 2012.

Paul Mason, *Why It's Kicking Off Everywhere: The new global revolutions*, Verso, 2012.

George Monbiot, 'The astroturf libertarians are the real threat to internet democracy', *The Guardian*, 13 Dec 2010, nin.tl/SwvqYK

Evgeny Morozov, *The Net Delusion: How not to liberate the world*, Penguin, 2012.

Carl Morris, 'Imagining the Welsh language web', *Global Voices*, 31 July 2012, nin.tl/UnD2mf

Richard Murphy, 'The courage to pay: Tax, faith, honesty and business', *Methodist Church in Britain* website, 2 Jul 2012, nin.tl/SwvHes

John Naughton, *A Brief History of the Future: The origins of the internet*, Phoenix, Orion Books, 2000.

John Naughton, 'Yet another Facebook revolution: Why are we so surprised?', *The Observer*, 23 Jan 2011, nin.tl/UnDq42

Jenny Pickerill, *Cyberprotest: Environmental activism online*, Manchester University Press, 2003.

Tariq Ramadan, *The Arab Awakening: Islam and the new Middle East*, Allen Lane, 2012.

Yasmine Ryan, 'How Tunisia's revolution began', Al Jazeera English website, 21 Jan 2011, nin.tl/Sww3BK

Richard Seymour, 'Quebec's students provide a lesson in protest politics', *Guardian* website, 7 Sep 2012, nin.tl/UnDDUJ

Gene Sharp, *From Dictatorship to Democracy*, Serpent's Tail, 2012.

Jessica Valenti, 'Slutwalks and the future of feminism', *Washington Post*, 3 Jun 2011, nin.tl/SwwhbS

Salma Yaqoob, 'Support the Slutwalk', Salma Yaqoob's blog, 17 June 2011, nin.tl/UnDW1W

Index

About New Internationalist

We are an independent not-for-profit publishing co-operative. We publish a monthly magazine and a range of books covering current affairs, education, world food, fiction, photography and ethical living, as well as customized products, such as calendars and diaries, for the NGO community.

New Internationalist magazine

Agenda: *cutting edge reports*

Argument: *heated debate between experts*

Analysis: *understanding the key issues*

Action: *making change happen*

Alternatives: *inspiring ideas*

Arts: *the best of global culture*

Print ✦ Digital ✦ New app for iPad

www✦newint✦org

Other World Changing titles from New Internationalist

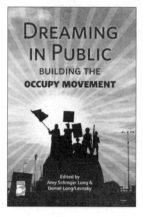

Among the growing range of books on the Occupy movement *Dreaming in Public* will stand out for one simple reason. It is of the movement, not about it.

This is a stunningly comprehensive compilation of primary sources, from public statements to engaged reportage, essays focused on analysis and strategy, and documentation of the visual culture of the movement.

Created by two New York-based Occupy movement participants, Amy Schrager Lang and Daniel Lang/Levitsky, the book includes contributions from a wealth of protagonists, including Barbara Kingsolver, Naomi Klein, Sara Paretsky, Lemony Snicket and Staughton Lynd.

Counterpower is the single idea which explains why social movements succeed or fail. It has helped win campaigns, secure human rights, stop wars and even bring down governments.

Why is it that some campaigns succeed while others fail? Is it luck, or is there a common strategy unifying those that have achieved their aim, and what can we learn from the past? In *Counterpower*, activist Tim Gee takes an in-depth look at the strategies and tactics that have contributed to the success (or otherwise) of some of the most prominent movements for change from India's Independence Movement to the Arab Spring.

Other World Changing titles from New Internationalist

People First Economics takes a long, hard look at the mess globalized capitalism is in, and shifts the focus back to where it belongs – putting the needs of people and the environment first.

Vanessa Baird and David Ransom have gathered a passionate group of writers, activists, leaders and thinkers to seize this opportunity to replace deep-rooted problems with well-founded solutions.

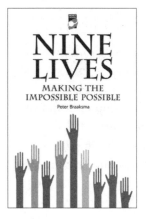

How do people keep going against all the odds in their efforts to change the world? *Nine Lives* introduces nine remarkable individuals who tell their own inspiring life stories and are blazing trails for others to follow.

From Cambodia to Israel-Palestine, nine stories from individuals standing up for their rights. 'You can cut the flower, but you cannot stop the coming of spring.' Malalai Joya, the young member of the Afghan parliament, refuses to let injustice go unchallenged. Her words reflect the irrepressible attitudes and actions of all the women and men who tell their stories here.